DEEP DOWN THINGS

LIN JENSEN

DEEP
DOWN
THINGS

The Earth in
Celebration and Dismay

WISDOM PUBLICATIONS

Wisdom Publications
199 Elm Street
Somerville MA 02144 USA
www.wisdompubs.org

Library of Congress Cataloging-in-Publication Data
Jensen, Lin.
 Deep down things : the earth in celebration and dismay / Lin Jensen.
   p. cm.
 Includes index.
 ISBN 0-86171-611-6 (pbk. : alk. paper)
 1. Nature—Religious aspects—Buddhism. 2. Human ecology—Religious aspects—Buddhism. I. Title.
 BQ4570.N3J46 2010
 294.3'5691—dc22
                         2010025724

14 13 12 11 10
5 4 3 2 1
eBook ISBN 978-0-86171-922-8

Cover design by Phil Pascuzzo. Interior design by LC. Set in Bulmer MT 12/16.

Earlier forms of five chapters herein have appeared in the following periodicals, websites, and anthologies: "Ten Hearts of an Earthworm" in *Tricycle*; "Roots" and "The Whole World Is Kin" posted as *Tricycle Web Exclusives*; "Digging Holes" posted on Powell's Books' website; "Buddhist Economics" in the anthology *A Buddhist Response to the Climate Emergency*.

To Joanna Macy
in gratitude for her tireless efforts
to preserve and protect the living earth

TABLE OF CONTENTS

ACKNOWLEDGMENTS

I THANK ALL THOSE who throughout the years have written and acted in defense of the earth, such as the Jesuit poet Gerard Manley Hopkins, Henry David Thoreau, Ralph Waldo Emerson, E.F. Schumacher, Arne Naess, George Sessions, Aldo Leopold, Annie Dillard, and Joanna Macy, and who have appeared in the pages of this book. And I thank as well others who haven't appeared herein but whose influence on my own environmental concerns and philosophy has been profound. Among these some of the most important are the brothers Ronald and Donald Culross Peattie, Wendell Berry, Francis Moore Lappe, Edward Abbey, Terry Tempest Williams, and Masanobu Fukuoka. And I'm thankful as well for the profound aspects of deep ecology that pervade the teachings of the Buddha and that have shaped a path of economic restraint and voluntary simplicity for myself and other Buddhists to follow. Once again I thank my wife, Karen Laslo, for her support and guidance not only in matters of writing but in life as well. Karen has shown kindness and forbearance in her toleration of the long hours and days I sometimes spend at a computer when an outbreak of writing has overtaken me. I also want to thank Josh Bartok, editor at Wisdom Publications, for his guidance in shaping this book in its finished form. This is the fourth book of mine that Josh has edited, and with each book my gratitude for his wisdom and insight deepens. Josh believes in what I'm doing and, more importantly, he understands what I'm doing. He knows where my strengths as a writer lie and where they do not. And when I've strayed away from the path I was meant to walk, he puts my feet back on home ground once more. Where else would I find an editor with the affection and courage to tell me to take a deep breath and hold on because he's about to suggest cutting three major chapters from a book of mine? After the lightning quits flashing and the thunder recedes and the wind dies down, and after I quit fretting over three months worth of discarded paragraphs and sentences, I'm invariably grateful to see that my writing is much the better for this tough love of his. Josh, I can't thank you enough.

EARTH:
AN INTRODUCTION

U NFORTUNATELY, I have some unavoidably bad news to
report regarding the state of the earth. It can't be helped.
It comes with the facts. The truth is we're poisoning the
planet with our industry, bringing uncountable other species to
extinction, and heating up the planet with potentially disastrous
consequences. It's enough to break the heart. It's not new. As long
as a century and a half ago the Jesuit poet Gerard Manley Hopkins,
residing in the coal-blighted suburbs of London, witnessed conditions much like our own:

> Generations have trod, have trod, have trod;
> And all is seared with trade; bleared, smeared with toil;
> And wears man's smudge and shares man's smell: the soil
> Is bare now, nor can foot feel, being shod.

Hopkins didn't flinch from the harsh truth of what he saw, but he saw as well another truth that might easily be overlooked:

And for all this, nature is never spent;
There lives the dearest freshness deep down things. . . .

I read these words here in a twenty-first century American town, and I take heart from the persistent tufts of grass and that inch their way up through cracks in the asphalt pavement of the street outside, and from the backyard dogwood tree that season after season ripens red berries for flocks of waxwings to feast upon. Everywhere I look, I see evidence of deep down things. I might never have become a Buddhist had I not first encountered Zen Master Dogen's *Tenzo Kyokan* or in English "Instructions to the Cook." It was the first Buddhist text I ever read, and it engaged me in such a way that I entered the path of Zen and never looked back. It's often said that while the *Tenzo Kyokan* gives literal instructions on how to cook, it's actually an analogue for how to live one's life whatever one happens to be doing. I don't doubt that Dogen's instructions can be profitably read that way, but the Tenzo (as the chief cook of a Zen monastery is called) actually spends his hours and days, sometimes years, devoted to the duties of the monastery kitchen and garden. The gardening and cooking of the monastery cook isn't metaphorical, it's actual. If I respect, honor, and value the rice and vegetables that come to hand and know how best to prepare them for use by the body, then I know what I most need to know of life. My kitchen work stands as it is without adjunct interpretation. The *Tenzo Kyokan* is earthy and rich with the growth, care, and use of living things. The work of kitchen and garden is a quintessential human exchange with land.

The nature of that exchange is of great concern to me, and this book was written in an effort to better understand the relationship between society and environment, between the people and land. A wealth of detail regarding specific interactions within an ecosystem is already being compiled through the systematic methods of inquiry utilized by the science of ecology. We humans are involved in that interaction, and what I'm after in this book is not so much the data but the condition of mind essential to a genuine human interaction with earth. What has been lost to us that we no longer know how to speak the language earth speaks? What have we forgotten to think or say or do that, could we but remember, would restore our acquaintance once more?

As both a Buddhist and a student of deep ecology, I'm struck by how much the two have in common, each exacting of the follower a genuine paradigm shift in perception. For the Buddhist the shift is an awakening to earth as an extension of one's own body wherein the dichotomy of self and other dissolves. For the deep ecologist the shift is a similar awakening wherein earth is realized as one indivisible body comprised of all beings of any sort. In both instances, this awakening is of profound proportions arguing for a shared communal relationship with earth that is unknown in modern industrial society. Of the eight principles of deep ecology as set down by Arne Naess and George Sessions, the seventh principle states the extent of the change required:

> The ideological change is mainly that of appreciating quality (dwelling in situations of inherent worth) rather than adhering to an increasingly higher standard of living. There will be a profound awareness of the difference between big and great.

For both the Buddhist and the deep ecologist, quality resides in dwelling itself. Anything that dwells—a stone, leaf, rabbit, the back yard elm tree, my next-door neighbor—has an inherent worth not derivative of its value to others. The quality of dwelling resides in its own stead and can't be valued on the market. The difference between big and great that Naess and Sessions cite lies in the fact that bigness is a comparative valuation based on quantity, while greatness comes large *or* small and its valuation exists outside comparison. In America, our higher standard of living is largely a matter of bigness, a standard external to the inherent quality of life itself. The insistence that the worth of a thing inheres in the thing itself and not in its value to others is what weds Buddhism to deep ecology and distinguishes deep ecology from the science of ecology in general. It's a perception that recognizes the right of all beings to exist simply because they do. Nothing is left out, nothing excluded.

In the pages that follow, I've written a great deal about farms and food because it is there in the orchards, fields, ranch lands, and kitchens of a nation that we humans enact an intimate and essential interaction with earth. But I also write a great deal about human culture and society itself. I can't reason intelligently about the land without including the humans who inhabit the land, particularly since I'm interested in the impact of the exchange between the two. I suppose that what has driven me more than anything else to write *Deep Down Things* is that in our society, such as it is now, we are often attending to things that are less and less deep down.

Long before I discovered its expression in Buddhism I felt the body of earth as though it were my own, just as you did. Just as we all do when we set aside false distinctions to the contrary. It's a love affair really, and one we need to take up again while the loved one is still responsive to our need. If such language seems excessively anthropomorphic, it might be that we've forgotten how reciprocal our relationship with earth actually is. We've forgotten that love of earth is a mutual exchange, a call and response, a giving and receiving from both sides.

I have written as much in celebration as in dismay, for it is my faith that there still lives "the dearest freshness deep down things." On the east side of town prime orchard land lies buried under Chico's South Mall, but on the west side of town the fields of a young and thriving organic cooperative are green with new life. My prayer is that to the very last of this planet's brief tenure in the vast cycle of the universe someone will remain to say "earth" and to say it from the heart's core.

ROOTS

We humans live a seesaw sort of life, going up only to come down again, going down in order to push back up.

INEED TO SAY SOMETHING OBVIOUS ABOUT ROOTS, namely that it's the root that supports the plant. Without roots, there'd be no leaves, blossoms, or fruit. This is the natural way of growth. I think we humans are like that too though we may at times fail to recognize our connection with what's under foot. What's under foot is earth itself, and while we possess the gift of locomotion, as say a tree does not, we are no less tethered to earth than is any plant. I'm a Buddhist, and I've always felt that it was the way of a Buddhist to put down roots like those of a tree and to draw life into oneself in that way. I thought that what Buddhists call wisdom is knowing how to connect dirt with sky. Even the highest mountain rests on the lower plain.

There's a story told about the Buddha that at the time of his enlightenment Mara, the Buddhist mythological embodiment of temptation, appeared with intent to undermine the Buddha's resolve. Mara challenged the Buddha to name by what authority he claimed enlightenment. The Buddha didn't name the authority of any god or prior teacher or mastery of any scripture; he simply touched a hand to the ground. That gesture has always seemed to me a peculiarly Buddhist expression of something deeply felt by nearly all we humans. We understand somehow that body and mind are born of earth, a maternal heritage that remains forever intact. And we know as well that when this mothering bond is broken, we wither and die like pulled weeds.

There's nothing in Buddhist philosophy like that of the biblical tradition granting humans "dominion over the fish of the sea, and over the fowl of the air, and over the cattle, and over all the earth, and over every creeping thing that creepeth upon the earth." Nor is there anything in Buddhist teaching that puts the *care* of earth in human hands. What the teaching actually does is put we humans in the care of *earthly* hands. We are the offspring of dirt and air and water, and no prideful boast to the contrary alters that. In my mind's eye I picture the Buddha sitting cross-legged on the ground. I like to think that earth somehow holds fast to him and secures him in the face of Mara's attempt to shake him loose. I like to think that when the Buddha put his hand to the ground that, in that single gesture, he pointed to the birthplace of his and all our lives, and thus could not be dislodged by the cleverest effort to bring him to doubt.

Given any chance at all, most children like to play in the dirt, sensing somehow an unspoken intimacy with earth. They seek low places, insinuating themselves into the dark beneath the limbs of trees, mashing down little clearings in patches of spring weeds as places to sit, in general soiling their clothes, staining their elbows green, and getting their hair gummy with dust and grit. After a night of rainfall, they ruin school shoes and splash mud up the backs of trousers and skirts stomping in mud puddles. Their mothers are forever telling them to clean their fingernails. These children somehow remember dwelling in the ground from which their lives so recently sprang. They hear the call from underneath and, in their innocent play, enact the journey home.

My wife Karen spent her childhood in a crowded little trailer park in San Fernando Valley, California. It remains to this day as it was when Karen was a child: not much more than a patch of gravel and dirt with trailers spaced row on row. When Karen took me there, I saw with my own eyes that she had grown up in a parking lot, devoid of trees or lawn or much of anything that would soften the stark bareness of the place, the single exception being an unpaved drainage canal that ran parallel to the property, its banks grown over with straggly grass and dotted with a few scrubby trees. It's here that Karen and the trailer-park children played. They were drawn to that patch of weeds and grass as though it were whipped cream on a pound cake. Not one of you reading this is likely to be surprised by that. That's what children do—give him or her a choice and it's a rare child that won't go for even the most pathetic surviving strip of residual nature in preference to acres of other paved options.

So Karen and her friends hung out in the hours after school on the grassy bank of the drainage canal. It was there that they ate their popsicles and ice cream bars from the vendor. And when sitting became tiresome, they rescued old cardboard boxes from the dumpster and slid down the slick grassy bank of the canal in these makeshift sleds. When the city sprayed the grass with herbicide and the children were told to stay off it, they fretted until allowed back again. They couldn't do otherwise. It was simply their nature to do as they did, an urging they responded to without exercising choice. Even the most withered and yellowed remnant of the natural world called them to return and that's what they did. If you bother to notice at all, you'll see that that's what most kids do and what you probably did once yourself.

I know it's what I did. In a patch of willows and cottonwoods on the banks of the Santa Ana River, a quarter mile from the farm where I lived as a small boy, lay the site of my own return to earth. On a warm day, the sun filtered down through the cottonwood canopy overhead onto a little clearing of sand swept clean by the river in seasons of high water. An undergrowth of willows encircled the clearing like the walls of a private room. I never brought anyone here. I was highly excitable as a boy and seldom still, yet there on the warm sand of my riverbank retreat I could sit in quiet reflection for periods stretching out to an hour or more. I seemed to tolerate my own company better there than I could anywhere else at the time. I once discovered the presence of a jack rabbit nearby, sitting perfectly still as I was, its large dark eyes seemingly focused on my own and, for the moment, the eyes of the rabbit were mirrors returning the reflection of my own face.

I was a precocious reader as a child, reading Wordsworth's *Lyrical Ballads*, Emerson's essays, Thoreau's *Walden*, and later such books as Le Comte du Nouy's *Human Destiny* with a surprising degree of youthful comprehension. My reading seemed to hold out a promise to me that, if I persisted, I would come to see my place and purpose in the world more clearly. I would turn the pages one after another, and the words I read held for me an appealing and yet frightening promise of heights as yet unvisited and I was left feeling elevated somehow, like a child hoisted unto his father's shoulders to see the parade go by. Both my reading and my riverbank solitude seemed born of a longing I could not have described, the direction of which seemed both up and down. And so I sometimes lay as flat to the earth as I could and let my mind drift upward through the overhead canopy. Holding fast to earth seemed to me then and still seems now the best position from which to view the skies.

Wordsworth wrote, "The child is father to the man." Doesn't

the child residing in the adult father's mind retain some teasing rec-
ollection of that earlier relationship when he was mentor to the man
he has become? When, of a weekend, this grown man has dug
around in the garden a bit or raked up some fall leaves and gone to
the shower with dirt caked under his nails, he might just remember
one of the lessons he once gave himself. And throughout the following week the smell of wet leaves and turned earth may reach him up
the forty-eight flights to his office complex calling him back to earth
below.

Our highest aspirations, like the highest tips of the tallest trees,
must of necessity remain rooted in the ground below. It's natural to
look upward as well as down, to reach for the heavens while
depending on the earth. We humans live a seesaw sort of life, going
up only to come down again, going down in order to push back up.
It's an intricate cooperation between rise and descend, and, while
the going up is good and the heights are grand, it's essential to come
back to earth again, back to our roots.

TEN HEARTS OF AN EARTHWORM

Am I not, like these bewildered creatures,
also caught out on the pavement?

O N DARK MORNINGS after nights of heavy rainfall, I find them stranded on the concrete sidewalk that leads to my front door and again later on the asphalt pavement that winds through the woods along Chico Creek. They know nothing of pavement, which doesn't figure in their knowledge of the world. They know dirt, leaf, root, air, and water. They are intimate with the ways in which decaying things rot into new life, a wisdom of which we who walk or ride along our various morning routes know so little. But caught out on an alien plain of concrete or asphalt, they inch along with little contractions and expansions of their segmented bodies toward certain death. If left exposed to even the palest sunlight, the UV rays of the sun will kill them. They will shrivel down to a crusty hardness, like a twisted twig or a stiffened length of discarded leather shoelace.

Entering my seventy-eighth year as I write this, I find I have time at my disposal to notice things. And if I really stop to look at the dozen or so earthworms that have chanced onto the sidewalk, I find

I can't leave them there to die. I must return them to the lawn or put them under a shrub or among the flowers somewhere. In Chico's Bidwell Park where they sometimes emerge onto the creek road by the hundreds, I can only save a few and must ultimately leave the rest to perish.

An earthworm is actually difficult to take hold of. Their bodies are coated with a lubricant that allows them to move smoothly along the little channels they form underground, and when you take hold of one, you'll find it's very slick and will easily slip from your fingers and fall back on the concrete. Not only that, but an earthworm's response to being touched is to wriggle and twist about in order to free itself.

I'm aware that a certain comic absurdity attends the image of an old man struggling to save the life of an earthworm that's fiercely resisting rescue. But seeing them there on the pavement stranded and perplexed by the loss of familiar habitat calls up my own loss of familiar ground, the fields and family farms of my youth given way to shopping malls and freeway interchanges. Am I not, like these bewildered creatures, also caught out on the pavement? It's not unreasonable to feel this way in a world encrusted with structures of our own invention, a world where so much of the natural order, rhythms, and textures of the living earth lie buried beneath the works of our own hands. It's not a new circumstance, of course, and it's not just about worms.

Here in the twenty-first century, under the guise of progress and development, we humans have built for ourselves a veritable maze of puzzling synthetic distractions to be negotiated. We're left in a circumstance like that of not knowing what to wear because the closet is hung with an array of garments so superfluous that none seems essential to our needs. Or we stand stymied in the supermarket breakfast food section staring blank and uncomprehending at box after box of contrived and unfamiliar offerings, searching for something corresponding to a natural appetite. Our lives are increasingly analogous to surfing the net or grabbing for the remote in search of a more stimulating channel to entertain ourselves with. We are statistics in the ratings, data for the advertisers. It's apparent to me that like those lost and stranded worms inching their way across the morning pavement toward death, we humans too are embarked on an errant and pointless journey toward our own eventual demise.

If you resist the comparison of human circumstances to those of the earthworms, you'll find that you already have more in common with them than you might at first suspect. I've learned that the earthworms I'm picking off the sidewalk, the ones occurring in the temperate zone of northern California's Central Valley, are of the species *Lumbricus terrestris*. A typical lumbricid, like we humans, has a brain, albeit a rudimentary one. And like us it has a heart, in fact ten hearts—five pairs that pump blood through a closed circulatory system like our own. And while it's true that earthworms eat dirt, it must be admitted that we do too. Since soil is the basis for all terrestrial plant life and thus of anything that can be eaten, can it not be said that I'm compelled to eat from the very dirt under my feet? And if the improbable transformation of sunlight to chlorophyll by way of photosynthesis is the critical support for the entire earthly food chain, don't the worms and I share an unavoidable appetite for sunlight as well? And don't I drink at the same fountain of snowmelt and rainfall? In fact, can't it be truly said that I eat the worms themselves, since their castings feed the plants upon which I in turn feed? That the worms and I and all creation are wrapped up with each other in a state of such inseparable interdependence is both a basic tenet of modern ecology and the primal structure and insight upon which Buddhist life and ethics are based.

I once came upon a surprising and arresting statement by Charles Darwin about the common earthworm: "It may be doubted whether there are any other animals which have played so important a part in the history of the world, as have these lowly creatures." I must have been fourteen or fifteen years old when I read this, but I somehow knew that what Darwin said of earthworms might well be said of any creature we humans share the earth with. I think I'd have to be willfully indifferent to fact if I were to suppose that I could include only those life forms to my liking and dispense with all the rest. Earthworms are particularly illustrative of the folly of ignoring the essential symbiotic relationship of all life. Yet I have found that there are people who simply loathe worms, are disgusted by them. Such people would be glad to be rid of the nasty things and would find my morning worm rescues little more than a quirky sentimentality that overtakes old men with a compromised capacity for realistic judgment.

My neighbor across the street has been waging a decades-long war with the worms in her lawn. She complains that they leave "unsightly" droppings on the lawn and that she's found no effective way to be rid of them. What's missing in her complaint is the fact that the reason her lawn stays so green and vibrant is because of the very earthworms she's been struggling all these years to exterminate. Earthworms are nature's preeminent composters. They convert dead organic matter into rich humus essential to the growth of healthy plants. It's this unseen, underground gardening of the worms that ensures the continuing cycle of soil fertility. Not only that, but earthworms "plow" the soil as well by tunneling through it. And these tunnels are the passageways through which air and water circulate. Soil microorganisms and plant roots need air and water just as we do. Without this vital work of the worms, soil would quickly compact to the point where air and water would no longer reach the roots of plants. Should this ever occur, we will watch helpless and perplexed as everything green turns gray, withers, and dies.

The most cursory investigation reveals that the continued healthy life not only of the earthworm but that of virtually all the earth's creatures is essential to the continued healthy life of humans as well. Yet it is not on the basis of benefits derived that Buddhist ecology takes its particular form. While the follower of the Buddhist path acknowledges her dependence on the whole ecosystem to sustain her own life, she nonetheless values the natural world with all its fellow beings, sentient and nonsentient, not for the personal benefit she derives from them but simply for their own sakes. This is a traditional Buddhist perception that accords with the contemporary perception of *deep* ecology. When Arne Naess, recognized as the founder of deep ecology, and his colleague George Sessions set down in writing the first three principles of their Deep Ecology Platform, they were stating principles already paramount in the life of a Buddhist:

1. All life has value in itself, independent of its usefulness to humans.
2. Richness and diversity contribute to life's well-being and have value in themselves.
3. Humans have no right to reduce this richness and diversity except to satisfy needs in a responsible way.

Nowhere that I know of in the long Buddhist canon will you find stated principles quite like these, yet they are principles that would seem perfectly familiar and self-apparent to those early followers of the Buddha 2,600 years ago.

When I stoop to rescue a stranded earthworm from the sidewalk, my doing so costs me nothing more than a moment's mindful attention. I only need to notice what is happening and act in accord with the obvious requirement of the moment. I do so simply because this little creature exists, its mere presence there on the sidewalk declaring its inherent right to its own life. And so when I finally get the thing in hand and drop it back on the lawn, the act may not seem to count for much in the larger scale of events; after all an acre of cultivated ground contains thousands of such worms. Yet in the very motion of reaching out and returning even a single earthworm to its rightful habitat, I enact the quintessential movement of twenty-six centuries of Buddhist ecology.

SIGHTING THE
MORNING STAR

*Once seen in its own right, the morning star
binds all life together in one inseparable body.*

IT IS TOLD that sitting meditation in the predawn hours of the morning the Buddha looked up and saw the morning star, a sight that occasioned his enlightenment. With the sun crawling up from the eastern mountains, he called out into the dawn, crying, "I am awakened together with the whole of the great earth and all its beings." All who follow the Buddha Way have read of that moment, seeing in the Buddha's pronouncement whatever registers in their own hearts. But for me his spontaneous outcry on sight of the morning star was the first and perhaps most penetrating revelation of the deep ecology that permeates Buddhist life, for the Buddha's enlightenment was itself a realization that he, the star, and the whole of the earth were manifestations of one being. He saw that the surface of his skin was not the termination of self and that the "I" for which he could no longer discern beginning or ending was as wide as the universe and as long as forever. The eye with which he looked upon the morning star was the one great organ of sight that awakens all our dawns.

The morning of the Buddha's awakening was a rare moment of seeing through the egocentric persuasion that dominates human thought, revealing his kinship with all beings. He would readily understand how the worms that inhabit my yard are kindred to me and how the sparrows, jays, and bluebirds that come to my fountain are extensions of my own being. At some level of comprehension we all know this, but our recognition of it gets lost in self-concern. We like to think we shape our lives and want to take credit for the outcome, touting our independence and willfully resisting the truth that we owe every breath we draw to forces and lives other than our own. The Buddha's awakening was more humbling than elevating, his long pursuit of truth ending in the ordinary, everyday truth of the moment; the enlightenment he'd so long sought turned out to be a common occurrence after all, shared by everything that swam, flew, walked, or crawled the earth with him, his very mind and body borrowed on loan from the dirt under his feet. Perhaps he saw his modest situation from the vantage of that far morning star, its light reaching him among the uncountable millions of lives he shared the dawn with.

If you care to notice, the morning star shines everywhere—in the eye of a child, in the faces of sunflowers tracking their namesake across the sky, in the sudden flash of trout feeding in the whitewater rapids, in the haunting mimicry of a mockingbird, in your own reflection in the bathroom mirror, and, yes, in the tracings of earthworms on fallen leaves. Once seen in its own right, the morning star binds all life together in one inseparable body. At whatever time and place you recognize its rising will be the very time and place of the Buddha's enlightenment.

If it is in the nature of enlightenment to awaken to a wider sense of self, then it's not surprising that such awakening occurs often and in the most unlikely circumstances. Arne Naess saw the source of the deep ecology movement to reside in what he called an ecological awakening to "wide identification." My own first hint of what Arne Naess meant by the term occurred when I was still a boy, years ago and long before I had even heard of Arne Naess or read a single word of his. My father was an immigrant farmer from Denmark who brought his own tradition of farming with horses to America, where we used them to work the fields and haul feed to a large flock of turkeys we raised. One of our horses was a powerful Belgian draft horse named Bill, an animal that I especially liked for his gentleness. It was on a day when I'd hitched Bill to a feed cart and was out feeding turkeys in a yard distant from the barns and house that the awakening Arne Naess spoke of paid me a brief visit.

I was given to occasional attacks of tachycardia, a racing heart, in those days and would often faint when such attacks occurred. It was late afternoon and I was scooping grain into the feeders when I felt the first irregular heart palpitations. Hungry turkeys were swarming about my legs, competing to get at the feed, and a few had hopped up into the cart to have a go at it there. Turkeys will peck at anything they can get at and I was suddenly afraid that if I passed out on the ground, they might peck at my eyes and I would awaken with empty sockets where sight once was. I thought of crawling up into the cart, but the birds could easily reach me there. And then I thought of the shades we'd put up for the birds on hot days, built like long arbors on eight-foot posts with turkey fencing stretched out on top and spread with loose alfalfa to block the sun. If I could make it up there somehow, I'd be okay. Getting dizzier and more breathless with each passing moment, I drove Bill toward the shade until he'd come alongside it and, with what strength was left me, I crawled up over the cart and onto Bill's back and up the powerful arch of his neck and pulled myself onto the safety of the shade, where I passed out.

I awoke to the creak of harness and the heavy thump of a hoof on the ground. "Bill?" He hadn't moved and from where I lay I could have reached out and touched his forehead with my hand. I'm not saying now—and I don't think I would have then—that Bill had waited there on my behalf. But there he stood, as trustworthy as a secured ladder, to help me climb back down. It was then that I felt his massive body as though it were my own. I felt the weight of the wagon tongue pulling the harness straps tight over my broad back, the flare of my nostrils drawing deep draughts of breath, the ripple of skin where the flies lit. For the instant, I was all draft horse. Bill was my morning star. I'd glimpsed the world of wide identification and I would find it difficult to ever put the eyes that had awakened to that reality back to sleep again.

Aldo Leopold's moment of wide identification left him "thinking like a mountain." In a chapter of his book, *A Sand County Almanac*, Leopold describes how it happened:

> We saw what we thought was a doe fording the torrent, her breast awash in white water. When she climbed the bank toward us and shook out her tail, we realized our error: it was a wolf. A half-dozen others, evidently grown pups, sprang from the willows and all joined in a welcoming melee of wagging tails and playful maulings. What was literally a pile of wolves writhed and tumbled in the center of an open flat at the foot of our rimrock.
>
> In those days we had never heard of passing up a chance to kill a wolf. In a second we were pumping lead into the pack, but with more excitement than accuracy; how to aim a steep downhill shot is always confusing. When our rifles were empty, the old wolf was down, and a pup was dragging a leg into impassable side-rocks.

We reached the old wolf in time to watch a fierce green fire dying in her eyes. I realized then, and have known ever since, that there was something known only to her and to the mountain. I was young then, and full of trigger-itch; I thought that because fewer wolves meant more deer, that no wolves would mean hunters' paradise. But after seeing the green fire die, I sensed that neither the wolf nor the mountain agreed with such a view.

For Leopold it was a moment wherein the distinction between his own mind and body and that of the wolf and mountain blurred and he took on the mind of the mountain itself. He looked into the green fire of the dying wolf's eyes as though into a mirror and saw his own reflection.

The earth calls us to awaken from our long night's isolated sleepwalk. Its call reached the Buddha in his meditation beneath the morning star, was heard by Arne Naess in the solitude of his simple cabin under the shadow of Norway's Hallngskarvet Mountain, spoke to Aldo Leopold in the language of a dying wolf's eyes, and even called a young boy from out of his child's sleep on a Southern California turkey farm.

It's obvious that you can't awaken the occupant of a household if no one's home. If the truth of the oneness of all beings had no residence in the human heart, no such truth could be roused to wakefulness. But if even a few give testimony to its presence among us, we can take heart in knowing that what's needed already lies latent within us and only needs to be called from its sleep.

And when it is, we awaken to the body of living earth again.

FOUR TRUTHS THAT SPARE THE EARTH

What I mean to say is that human law is bound by natural law and that earth itself speaks the truth of the human condition.

TRADITION HAS IT that the first teaching of the Buddha was that of the four noble truths, and that everything he taught afterward was a footnote to that first teaching. The Buddha's discourse of the four noble truths lands us squarely in the context of earthly life, revealing the source of the peculiarly human distress and suffering that so disrupts earth's inherent integrity and balance. We're told that this first talk was given to five ascetic monks with whom the Buddha had previously trained. He explained to them what he had discovered regarding the nature of suffering, its causes, and the means to bring it to an end. He told the five ascetics, "I did not claim before to have awakened to unsurpassed perfect enlightenment, but when knowledge and vision of these four noble truths was given me, then I claimed to have awakened to unsurpassed perfect enlightenment."

The Buddha, however, didn't claim these truths were of his own invention. He could spell them out in four reasoned steps, but the source of these steps was a timeless wisdom that predated his or

anyone else's discovery of them. He once described the path leading to the cessation of suffering as an "ancient road traveled by the
perfectly enlightened ones of the past." When the Buddha gave his
first discourse on the four noble truths, he wasn't offering an opin-
ion to the ascetics; he was passing on a law of the universe.

For a student of ecology who is also intimate with the four noble
truths, this universal law of human suffering is itself grounded in the
natural law of an earthly ecosystem. An obvious example would be
the realization of impermanence embedded in the four noble truths
as consistent with the constant shift and recycling of the earth's
material components. I don't mean by such example to merely suggest how readily one can find analogies between the laws that govern nature and the laws that govern human suffering or how easily
one can compose similes illustrative of that connection. What I
mean to say is that human law is bound by natural law and that earth
itself speaks the truth of the human condition. My particular interest is in the implications of the four noble truths for human social,
political, and environmental impact upon earth.

Bhikkhu Bodhi, the renowned translator of Pali, in his anthology called *In The Buddha's Words*, has arranged the Buddha's
teaching of the four noble truths against a backdrop of the human
conditions under which suffering occurs. Among these conditions
are the obvious and unavoidable natural fact of aging and death. In
a dialogue between the Buddha and King Pasenadi of Kosala, the
Buddha composes an extravagant simile in which he likens the
inevitability of loss, decay, and eventual death to an image of
encroaching mountains high as the clouds coming from every side
to crush all humanity under their irresistible force and weight.
Then he asks the king, "If such a great peril should arise, such a terrible destruction of human life, what should be done?" The king,
acknowledging the unavoidable suffering that awaits us all,

answers, "If such a great peril should arise, such a terrible destruction of human life, what else should be done but to live by the Dharma, to live righteously, and to do wholesome and meritorious deeds?'"

The Buddha's mountain simile is no exaggeration of the crushing force of greed, hatred, and delusion that threatens the stability and peace of his own time as it does now of ours. The destructive consequences arising from greed, hatred, and delusion seem painfully familiar to me here in the year 2009, and King Pasenadi's choice to live by the Dharma, righteously and wholesomely, seems as good a response as ever. The foremost dharma of the Buddhist Way is that of the four noble truths, a teaching that reconciles one to the natural laws of earthly existence.

The first of the four noble truths states the simple fact that suffering exists, an accurate enough description of the human circumstance. The Buddha lists some of the forms suffering takes. Birth itself, he says, involves suffering; old age, illness, and death bring suffering; not getting what you want is suffering; getting what you don't want is suffering; losing something or someone you care about is suffering; being stuck with something or someone you don't like is suffering, and so on. One can easily add to the list. As the Buddha says, we don't always get what we want. If we find such conditions unsatisfactory, then we'll find life itself unsatisfactory, because these *are* the conditions of our existence.

What the Buddha intends in his statement of the first noble truth is not that suffering is something gone wrong with the world, a problem to be fixed, but that suffering is rather a universal circumstance of planetary life. For me this was good news, confirmation of my own observation and experience of the life around me. I reasoned that, if some degree of suffering was inevitable, then my suffering was not necessarily a problem. I could accept things as they were and thereby quit arguing with circumstance and fall into harmony with life around me. I saw my own conditions reflected in the passing of the seasons, the sprouting of spring grasses, the blossoming of summer flowers, the fall of autumn leaves, the dark rest of winter. Things all about me came and went—birth, growth, maturation, procreation, aging, and death. The natural rhythms of the world matched my own passage through life. When I was able to recognize these conditions as a universal harmony of earthly existence, I was left without regret or grasping of the sort I'd once felt and was more content to be as I was among all the other nameless beings with which I share the earth. "Suffering exists," the Buddha said, and I knew from those reassuring words that I needn't resist.

The truth of suffering writes itself in impermanence on the face of the living earth where change comes with the swiftness of the hurricane or with the slow grind of the glacier on granite mountaintops. We see our mothers and fathers, and sometimes our children, disappear through death's door, reminding us that we will soon follow. If I struggle against these unavoidable conditions I will only suffer all the more. Realizing the universality of suffering softens the heart toward one's fellow creatures. Even a roadside patch of spring weeds hanging limp and desiccated from herbicide poisoning evokes a kindred recognition. Sympathies expand and, in that way, suffering summons its own healing. The truth of suffering recognizes the most apparent feature of an earthly ecosystem—namely that we're all in it together.

In the second noble truth, the Buddha lays out the origin of suffering. We suffer, he tells us, because of our clinging, our craving, our greed and attachment to what we want and our aversion to what we don't want. Can anyone doubt that it's precisely these likes and dislikes of ours that most cause us to suffer and bring unwarranted suffering to bear upon earth?

Summarizing the truth of suffering, the Buddha told the ascetics, "In brief, the five aggregates of existence subject to clinging are suffering." The *five aggregates* are an analysis of what constitutes human experience, the psycho/physical factors that condition our experience of ourselves and our surroundings. According to this analysis, all human experience consists of *consciousness* accessed by way of the six sense organs of eye, ear, nose, tongue, body, and, in Buddhism, mind. In turn, this consciousness is one of *bodily form*, ours and that of the world itself; *feeling*, sensations and the affective qualities of experience; *perception*, the identification and recognition of objects; and *mental formations*, the thoughts we generate in regard to objects. It's easy to trace the progression of these five aggregates toward clinging.

Suppose I'm pumping along on my seventy-seven-year-old legs, heading downtown on my thirteen-year-old $139 Hampton Cruiser bicycle, when a twenty-year-old youth passes me heading for classes at the university on a bicycle of his own. Now my consciousness of all this reaches me through my sense organs and is initially one of bodily form—of my body, the college youth's, and the two bicycles. My consciousness also consists of perception in that I recognize the object the youth is astride as a state of the art Ellsworth Oracle bicycle worth more than the trade-in value of the car parked in my garage at home. My consciousness is also one of feeling, and here we reach the point at which the aggregates are subject to clinging. Whereas before I was content to peddle along on my Hampton Cruiser, now I'm not so sure considering the comparative desirability of our two bikes. And whereas I was okay with the limits of my aging body, now I'm less so seeing this boy sailing effortlessly past me in casual conversation on a cell phone. My consciousness has now more or less converted to mental formation, a thought. And the thought is one of preferring this youth's bike and body to my own. My entire suffering, every tiny irritating itch of dissatisfaction, consists entirely of these thoughts. Clearly the five aggregates are subject to clinging just as the Buddha said they were, and in making that observation he points directly to the human predilection toward the greed that breeds dissatisfaction.

I wouldn't labor this if the nature of how we *experience* our surroundings weren't so critical an element in how we *interact* with our surroundings. It's no stretch of actual fact to see how such craving and attachment, often collective in nature, leads whole nations to plunder their weaker counterparts in quest of resources to add to their own. Armies are amassed and wars are fought over oil reserves. Corporations extract wealth and resources from vulnerable populations leaving the poor with no viable means of livelihood. Whole ranges of Appalachian mountaintops are blown apart by coal extractors to get at the coal underneath. Powerful agribusinesses, in their greed for control and profit, decimate whole countrysides of family farms. The Buddha himself once explained to his attendant, Ananda, how possessiveness leads to niggardliness and niggardliness leads to defensiveness resulting in "the taking up of clubs and weapons, conflicts, quarrels, disputes, insults, slander, and falsehood."

At the heart of all this greed is a false sense of self that feels somehow enhanced by possession, whether that is the possession of a new bike or an oil field. What's actually clung to is always a mental formation, an idea of some sort. And in that sense, we originate our own suffering. It might be said that we *think* our suffering into existence. It's the craving that does the harm and not the conditions of life, the craving that constitutes human suffering. Craving is a frame of mind wherein preference breeds aversion, and greed calls up hatred; a mind wherein like and dislike prevail. This craving gives rise to an erroneous perception of a separate self, the existence of which is anxiously reinforced by the sensual pursuit of material pleasures and goods. And this behavior persists despite the fact that only the most fleeting pleasure ever accrues from such pursuit and no lasting good is obtained at all.

The cost to the earth and human happiness brought on by this craving for self-assurance through sensual gratification has been immense. If continued unabated, it stands to destroy the balance of earth's ecosystem. Just since 1932, the year of my birth, I have witnessed in a single generation a comprehensive human disconnection with earth of a scale I could not have imagined as a boy. We have forgotten where we live and upon what we depend. Our ambitions outstrip our material supports and we are left without a secure home for either mind or body.

Considering the long course of human craving with its attendant suffering, it might seem hopeless to ever bring such suffering to a cessation. But the Buddha taught that there are two forms of suffering, which he likened to being struck by two darts. The first dart is the dart of *actual* pain, the pain of physical injury, illness, death, the loss of something or someone loved. In time, one or more of these will happen to each of us, and it will hurt. The second dart is mental and consists of the suffering comprised of how we *react* to the actual pain of physical injury, illness, death, the loss of something or someone loved. Our own hand throws this second dart of mental suffering, and it's in restraint of that peculiarly human self-injury that the truth of the Buddha's teaching of the cessation of suffering resides:

> Now this, monks, is the noble truth of the cessation of suffering: it is the remainderless fading away and cessation of that same craving, the giving up and relinquishing of it, freedom from it, nonattachment.

It was when this, the third of the four noble truths, had fallen in place, that Kondanna, one of the five ascetics grasped, the teaching in its entirety, saying, "Whatever is subject to origination is subject to cessation." At this, the Buddha, previously uncertain that the Dharma would ever be understood, cried out, "Kondanna understands! Kondanna indeed understands!" What Kondanna understood was how events unfold in mutual reciprocity. He understood that cause and effect are co-arising, that no cause arises without its effect arising with it and that no cause ceases without its effect ceasing with it. Cause and effect ride on each other's backs; when one moves, the other moves.

Kondanna understood this and we need to understand as well. We need more than ever to realize that what's done can be undone, simply by not doing what we're doing. And while to undo the mess we're making of our lives and of our earth is not so simple as clicking the "undo" in the word processor with which I'm typing these words, it is nonetheless within our human capacity, as Kondanna realized, to do so. We must initiate for ourselves the fading away and cessation of personal and communal craving; we must give it up, relinquish it, discover the freedom of nonattachment. So long as we are driven by willful desire, we will find that it has no capacity for self-limitation. Craving breeds its own kind; the thirst for more is self-perpetuating.

That origination is subject to cessation is the core logic of karmic consequence. If I can do harm, I can cease from doing harm. I can choose, and wherever choice is involved I'm held accountable for my actions. Since the suffering I originate is also subject to cessation, I alone hold the ethical responsibility for what I originate. And if I choose to continue along the path of greed, hatred, and delusion, then greed, hatred, and delusion will be the suffering I inherit of my own volition. It's the law of karma, and while karma may sound like a peculiarly Buddhist notion, it is in fact a simple and verifiable truth of human circumstance.

I've been at pains to demonstrate that social and environmental attitudes and behaviors are inseparably linked in communal collaboration between people and earth. And I've been further concerned to demonstrate that the Buddha's teaching of the four noble truths serves to identify the point at which this collaboration breaks down. Our species has acquired tremendous power for support or disruption of the ecosystem. We have mostly specialized in disruption, and the four noble truths points to the source of that grave error. Our survival requires that we give up the quest for individual self-promotion and personal profit. It's a misguided direction that only threatens the stability of the earthly ecosystem that alone sustains us.

What I want from this life as much as anything I've ever wanted is for we humans to spare each other the suffering we bring upon ourselves and upon the earth. I have found a means for doing this in the Buddha's fourth noble truth that sets forth an eightfold path leading to the cessation of our self-imposed human suffering. Of all the steps of the eightfold path, none has been more helpful to me than that of right intention:

> And what, monks, is right intention? Intention of renunciation, intention of good will, intention of harmlessness: this is called right intention.

If my intention is to win at the expense of another, there's a good likelihood that the competition will end up with a winner and a loser. To change that familiar outcome I must intend differently. Right intention does this by renouncing craving, and the attendant ill will and harm that attaches to such craving, and substituting in their stead generosity, good will, and harmlessness. If I look directly at what goes most astray and suffers most in human social and environmental behaviors, could I find a practice more suited to our present need than this very practice of right intention? To the extent that I can curb my desire for self gain and cultivate in its stead a little modesty, and to the extent that I can redirect whatever argument I might be having with circumstance toward a more understanding, patient, and affectionate regard, to that extent will I spare the world unnecessary harm.

EARTH LINEAGE

For me, an equivalent to the Pali Canon of Indian Buddhism is a canon of teachings in English that inquires into the human relationship to land.

O F C O U R S E , there's always the traditional Buddhist lineage in which the Buddha mind is passed from teacher to student. This *passing* of Buddha mind is actually an *acknowledgement* of the presence of Buddha mind already residing in another. Soto Master Houn Jiyu Kennett, Abbess of Shasta Abbey, once bowed to me and said, "Buddha bows to Buddha, Buddha recognizes Buddha." With that recognition, I'd inherited a lineage of Buddhist ancestry reaching from the time of Shakyamuni Buddha down through the centuries, which, by virtue of the Houn Jiyu's acknowledgement, now included me. I was taken thereby into a family that extended beyond my own individual genetic one and was given a scroll, which when opened revealed in generational sequence the names of eighty-five ancestral teachers of the Soto Zen lineage. The last name on the list was that of Houn Jiyu, followed by the notation "Lin Jensen, New Ancestor."

I've always treasured this little document, for I can recite any or all of the ancestors listed there, knowing that each of them has received the very same refuges and precepts as I have, and that all have held them in good order so that they might be passed on to others such as me. This lineage is called the bloodline of the Buddhas, the veins of which are the precepts of moral and ethical behavior. It's no casual thing to receive the precepts, for they constitute a lifetime vow that can't be fulfilled without the utmost sincerity and devotion to purpose. I'm humbled by the generations of ancestral teachers who, in an attitude of joy and gratitude, devoted themselves to the precepts long before I knew that such even existed.

What I want to acknowledge here is another lineage, an earth lineage that exists outside the formal framework of traditional Buddhist lineage and for which I'm equally grateful. Among these is a personal lineage of teachers who brought a knowledge of earth home to me. Many I've met solely through books they've written, though putting it that way suggests that an encounter by way of a book is somehow less intimate than an encounter in person. But anyone who has read much can attest to an intimate meeting of mind and heart between writer and reader that sometimes goes deeper than is reached in any other way, even in the daily exchange one has with family and friends.

For me, an equivalent to the Pali Canon of Indian Buddhism is a canon of teachings in English that inquires into the human relationship to land. It's an ancestry of earth literature that includes writings as disparate in time and kind as that of the Middle English *Piers Plowman*, in which Piers, the humble plowman of the title, appears and offers himself as a guide to the truth, passing through such works as Henry David Thoreau's mid-nineteenth century *Walden* down to such contemporary teachings as those of Annie Dillard's *Pilgrim at Tinker Creek*. Just as every Buddhist scripture or koan, regardless of its discrete content, is invariably about what

Buddhists term essential nature or Buddha nature, so too do these writers of earth scripture reach through and beyond the specific content of their works to give voice to the essential nature of our human exchange with earth.

Piers Plowman was written somewhere between 1360 and 1387 by a Middle English poet, William Langland, a contemporary of Geoffrey Chaucer. I first read this long narrative verse poem at Stanford University while studying under a fellowship. I was still fresh from a life of farming, and perhaps that's what accounts for my attraction to a poem that finds ultimate virtue in the life of the land. In the poem, Christ has reappeared as the humble plowman Piers.

Like Christ, Piers spoke on behalf of the poor: those who farmed the acres of the landed gentry, those who crafted the essential goods, swept out the stables, and cleaned the houses of the rich, those who had little and made do with what life offered. I discovered Langland's poem one afternoon in the rare books section of Stanford's library and read it in its entirety seated at a little alcove desk by a window there in the stacks. Will, the narrator in the poem, along with a knight, and an assembly of townsfolk comprised of housewives, milkmaids, carpenters, wheelwrights, farmers, and such were on a quest for Truth with a capital "T." It was a religious quest actually, and what they wanted to know was how best to conduct their lives so as to bring themselves in accord with what they thought of as heaven's enduring values. It was then that Piers the plowman came upon them, and turned their thoughts from the sky toward the earth with which they were already so intimate. The little group questioned Piers regarding their quest for truth because despite his apparent lowly and common stature, he possessed a composed and assured presence of person that encouraged them to hope he might be the bearer of the very Truth they sought. So they asked for the Truth.

Sitting there in the Stanford library stacks that afternoon, I don't know what heavenly advice I expected to hear from Piers, but what he told these truth seekers found its way into my heart and gave voice and shape to something I already carried within. Piers told them to "sew the sack to keep the wheat from spilling." He told them to "spin wool and make flax." "Conscience," he said, "counsels you to make cloth to benefit the poor and for your own sustenance." And then he added, "For I shall see to their sustenance, unless the land fail." "Help him live," he said, "who obtains your food." The knight at this point spoke of his regret that he knew nothing of plowing and working the land. And Piers told him, "I shall toil and sweat and sow for us both, and labor for those you love all my lifetime."

Piers Plowman, Langland's Christ of fourteenth-century England, was a common field laborer. The Truth he brought to those who sought truth was the truth of necessity, the truth of the essential interaction with earth. The scripture he wrote was the scripture of love's labor, the back bent to the task of bringing forth the miracle that springs from the soil under foot. Is this too simple a religion to credit with our salvation? Ask yourself that now when earthly disregard and misdirection threatens us on all sides. We could do a lot worse than adopt a religion that puts its faith in tilling the earth. Dirt is our proper heaven.

Thoreau, like Piers so many centuries before him, found faith in tilling the soil. In *Walden* he wrote, " I went to the woods . . . to front the essential facts of life," and he found those essential facts in the cultivation of a few acres of beans, peas, and potatoes. When the weeds began to take hold, Thoreau realized he'd planted too many bean rows and found it to be a daily labor just to keep the weeds down. "What was the meaning of this, so steady and self-respecting, this small Herculean labor, I knew not," he wrote. But then, despite the extent of the task, Thoreau confessed, "I came to love my rows, my beans, though so many more than I wanted. They attached me to the earth, and so I got strength like Antaeus." Thoreau has got it exactly right here. Antaeus of Greek mythology was famous for the great strength he derived from his mother, Gaia, the earth. He could defeat even Hercules as long as he remained in contact with the ground.

It was from this same immediate contact with the earth, the literal physical proximity of seeding, hoeing, and harvesting, that Thoreau drew new strength. And this was not strength of body alone that the earth passed on to him, but strength of spirit as well. It led Thoreau to ask, "What shall I learn of beans or beans of me?" And then, perhaps unwittingly, he answered his own question, "I cherish them, I hoe them, early and late I have an eye to them; and this is my day's work." I ask myself, what sweeter consequence could there be than finding my day's work?

Thoreau termed himself "a very *Agricola laboriosus*," a field laborer, a tiller of the soil. He liked to walk his bean rows barefoot. He must have known a naked dependence upon earth of a sort that we, in our high-rise condominiums far from the fields that succor us, so often forget. We lose the connection because the essential labor is so often done by proxy in a field remote from our presence. And when that persists, we lose our source of strength like Antaeus who, when deprived of contact with the ground, was crushed by Hercules' overpowering force.

In nearby Concord, Thoreau's contemporary Emerson wrote his remarkable essay, "Nature."

Here [in nature] is sanctity which shames our religions, and reality which discredits our heroes. Here we find Nature to be the circumstance which dwarfs every other circumstance, and judges like a god all men who come to her.

And then again in a later passage, Emerson acknowledges, as Buddhists have done for centuries, the seamless bond between all manifestations of being, human or otherwise:

We come to our own, and make friends with matter, which the ambitious despise. We never can part with it; the mind loves its old home: as water to our thirst, so is the rock, the ground, to our eyes and hands and feet.

Emerson would have us know that nature itself is the abiding teacher that ever brings to us the dharma of earth:

Every moment instructs, and every object: for wisdom is infused into every form. It has been poured into us as blood; it convulsed us as pain; it slid into us as pleasure; it enveloped us in dull, melancholy days, or in days of cheerful labor; we did not guess its essence until after a long time.

Perhaps it *has* been a long time coming, but there have been those, like Emerson and Thoreau, who did guess the essence of the moment in which wisdom is infused into form and have thus prepared for such as me an articulated dharma of earth as witness to what they found. Wisdom is manifest in the very stuff of the earth, and that realization draws our eyes back from the heavens to look out upon the surrounding landscape. We find our way through life by consulting what lies at hand. What can this rock, leaf, moth, field of grass teach me?

It was E.F. Schumacher in his book *Small Is Beautiful: Econom-*

ics As If People Mattered who first taught me to see how critical the scale of our economics is to the relationship we humans have with work. He saw that the advent of assembly-line manufacture was a soul-destroying enterprise in which work was divided up into disparate and meaningless segments where no worker experienced the construction of the whole. Just hammer in your five rivets as the chassis passes by; never mind the hours and years that are spent without you ever witnessing the car take shape in its entirety; clock out, pick up your pay check; buy yourself some fun on the weekend. Schumacher grasped the heart of Buddhist economics, which honors all activity as Buddha's activity, and sees work as essential practice. He would not have us expand an enterprise to the point where we can no longer bring the whole of it into view.

And then, as in any religious practice, Buddhist or otherwise, there's an area of the unknown requiring of us a respectful modesty that acknowledges the mystery of our lives. I have among the books I keep at hand a copy of Annie Dillard's *Pilgrim at Tinker Creek* so worn that the image on the cover of the book showing Annie seated at the creekside is so faded and worn as to be something of a mystery itself. But her whole book, every chapter, is rich with the wonder of an earth of unknown origin—not entirely unknown of course in its material origins, but an earth in which speculations regarding its spiritual origins leave us with more doubt than certainty. Annie's words restore me to proper doubt and return me to the mystery of earth. "We don't know what's going on here," she wrote. "We don't know. Our life is a faint tracing on the surface of mystery, like the idle, curved tunnels of leaf miners on the face of a leaf. We must somehow take a wider view, look at the whole landscape, really see it. . . . Then we can at least wail the right question into the swaddling band of darkness, or, if it comes to that, choir the proper praise."

Langland, Thoreau, Emerson, Schumacher, and Dillard are just a few of the generations of earth writers that figure importantly for me in my own personal earth lineage. Other writers and books are equally significant in their own ways: Colin Fletcher's *The Man Who Walked Through Time*, Wendell Berry's *Home Economics*, Edward Abbey's *Desert Solitaire*, and such fictional works as Sarah Orne Jewett's *The Country of the Pointed Firs* and Sue Monk Kidd's *The Secret Life of Bees*. But there are other teachers of earth dharma that have simply walked into my life from the most unlikely directions and who are unknown as such by anyone other than myself. Some of their teachings are of so simple and literal a nature that they might seem of little or no significance. Yet the most unlikely person and event may occasion the very dharma most needed.

One such occasion occurred when I was attempting to grow vegetables in Sierra Valley, a high mountain valley with a cold climate and short growing season in which a hard freeze could occur any month of the year. When the locals saw what I was up to, they told me, "Forget it. It can't be done." And in truth I couldn't find a single garden in the valley that appeared even remotely successful. But when I voiced my disappointment to Ron McCaffrey who'd been born and raised in the valley, he said his mother, Edith, had been keeping a garden there for years. I checked it out, and sure enough, there was Edith McCaffrey's garden filled with rows of lettuce, carrots, broccoli, cabbage, peas, potatoes, squash, and even a half dozen tomato plants hung heavy with ripening fruit. How had she done it under such difficult circumstances, I asked her. "I learned," was her answer. Before I left, she handed me a worn and yellowed notebook with entries in it. "You can borrow this," she said. "It might be helpful."

That evening, when I looked into Edith McCaffrey's notebook, I saw that it was a detailed journal of her experiences in gardening. The first entry was dated 1959. I was reading the journal in 1989. What I'd been given was thirty years of gardening in Sierra Valley. It was as if I'd found a previously unknown sutta of the Buddha's teachings. Edith McCaffrey was the teacher I most needed at the time, the first teacher of the ancestral lineage of Sierra Valley gardening. I stood to be the second. Edith's own teacher was earth itself. Everything she knew about gardening had been taught her by the dirt in her backyard. I may seem to be making a big deal out of a couple of inconsequential gardens in a mountain valley, but agriculture on any scale is an intimate exchange between teacher and disciple wherein earth itself is the ancestral teacher whose lineage dates back to the birth of a solar system.

HAVING THE LAKE
TO OURSELVES

*"We've caught fish and have buttered potatoes to
go with it. Why don't you join us?"*

SYMPATHY IS A CONSEQUENCE OF INCLUSION, the affectionate result of an expanded identity that occurs when
"self" and "other" is recognized as simply "self." The presence of this newly inclusive sympathetic connection relaxes bound-
aries and discloses a frame of mind that lets more in. I can best
explain this by example.

For several summers, my daughter Krista and I backpacked into
the most remote areas of Sierra Nevada Range where we could be
alone. We'd leave the trails and, traveling by compass, climb into
some high glacial cirque where the topographical map indicated
the presence of a lake. And if we found no one else there, we were
pleased to have the lake to ourselves. We felt a little proprietary and
even exclusive in a way, fishing the lake with no one but the two of
us rippling the still waters, hearing only the sounds of our own
voices, owning the whole view of the lake without a single intrusion
of someone's red, blue, or yellow tent anywhere to be seen with the
exception of our own.

We liked the sense we had of entering an unoccupied wilderness and seeing it as if we were the first ever to come that way. Yet we never quite felt relaxed in our solitude until night had fallen because other campers could show up at any time and spoil our good fortune. We'd set conditions that couldn't be enjoyed even when met. A worrisome little distress invariably accompanied having the place to ourselves. And, in addition, it sometimes felt quite selfish to wish for ourselves what we hoped to exclude for others.

This came to a head on a late afternoon at a lake in the Kern River watershed. Krista and I had climbed to 11,000 feet that day and found there a perfect setting. The lake lay still as a mirror reflecting the granite peaks that encircled the basin. The shoreline was dotted with miniature furs and there, in the high altitude spring of late July, the basin grasses were freshly green. The skies were clear with a bright, slanting sun, and night promised a full moon. We were setting up our tent and laying out the supper things, when I saw the two of them with their packs, laboring their way up the outlet stream toward the lake. I felt just that first twinge of mixed disappointment and shame, but this time I was moved to do something I'd never thought to do before. They were a couple, husband and wife I supposed, and having seen our campsite, they veered away from us, straining under the weight of their packs to reach a stretch of shoreline distant from our own. Perhaps they thought to respect our privacy—or theirs. But I intercepted them on their way. "My daughter and I were just getting supper started," I told them. "We've caught fish and have buttered potatoes to go with it. Why don't you join us?"

They did. And when they were included, the distinction between "we" and "they" readily dissolved. These "intruders" on our solitude turned out to be such good companions that I drifted into an easy and natural sympathy with them. We ate together like one family and watched the full moon rise over the basin. Our evening together brought home to me how the pronouns we humans choose to use are indicative of how we identify relationships, and before the four of us crawled into our sleeping bags that night, we'd commented (without apparent perception of irony!) on how fortunate it was that "we" had the lake all to ourselves.

It's imperative that we learn to share the earth. The reluctance to share what we have with "outsiders" is an attitude that worsens the ecological crisis we find ourselves in now. It often manifests as an anxious concern regarding available resources, a worry that breeds competition between us, and erodes sympathetic concern for the needs of others. But it also erodes sympathetic concern for earth itself and distracts us from recognizing the cooperative nature of the ecosystem, a cooperation that sustains all earthly life. It's an irony of the behavior of those who hoard and covet, that it's inherent in the very nature of things that we best help ourselves by helping others.

I don't think most people intend to deprive others of their rightful place and share in the world; it's just that in wanting the lake to ourselves, we forget that there are only so many lakes to go around.

GETTING RID
OF THE RABBITS

A relative peace settled on the farms that adopted these measures of accommodation and a sympathetic accord grew.

IF YOU'RE DEPENDENT ON FOOD from your own backyard garden and a horde of wild rabbits are getting to it first, it's not hard to understand that you'd want to get rid of the rabbits. I've seen this little drama of exclusion played out in the behavior of the farming families among whom I once lived. Our farms were located near the Santa Ana River where the overgrown banks gave cover and concealment to a population of rabbits numbering in the hundreds. Those of us with farms strung along the river and even those whose farms lay a mile or more distant from it were plagued with hungry rabbits who'd eat anything we managed to grow. These rabbits were mostly a minor and manageable hardship to those with large enough acreages planted in lima beans, alfalfa, and various vegetable row crops. But they could really cut into the harvest one anticipated from the kitchen gardens we all grew. The combination and variety of leafy greens and soft ripening vegetables concentrated in one place was an irresistible attractant to any rabbit hungry enough to venture that close to human habitation and try to snatch a quick meal before being caught or chased off by the yard dog. But for all the hazards, there were plenty of candidates willing to take the risk.

A kitchen garden served a need equivalent to today's supermarket produce sections. Homegrown food was essential to the economy of every farm household up and down the river. Most families did everything they could to get rid of the rabbits. They trapped rabbits, shot rabbits, poisoned rabbits, and staked out dogs so mean they were a threat to their own children. A few even tried to discourage the rabbits with ingenious clanging devices that produced a loud and irritating noise, but most of these inventions were perfectly silent unless the wind was strong enough to activate them and if that happened to be at night, which is when most rabbits feed, no one in the house could get any sleep. Not only that, but the rabbits didn't seem to mind the noise at all. And so after a number of farm dogs were inadvertently caught in rabbit traps and some others poisoned by rabbit baits, and after it became clear that no amount of rabbits shot, poisoned, or trapped was appreciably decreasing their numbers or the extent of their damage, it became clear to some—mostly the women of the household—that trying to rid themselves of the rabbits was not working.

Rabbits will eat leaf lettuce and other garden greens in preference to almost anything else if they're available. And so at some of the farms, the women, being the primary tenders of the kitchen garden, began to plant additional rows of such greens. The idea was that if the rabbits wanted greens, let them have greens. They'd simply grow enough to feed both the rabbits and themselves. It worked, not perfectly, but well enough so that these small sacrifices made on behalf of the rabbits' welfare didn't jeopardize the welfare of the farm. A relative peace settled on the farms that adopted these measures of accommodation and a sympathetic accord grew between rabbits and residents. In time, when the rabbits realized that they were no longer outsiders and weren't going to be shot at or poisoned or trapped or chased down by a vicious dog, you could sometimes find them in broad daylight nibbling greens in the garden with the housewife hanging out wash nearby and the farm dog asleep in the shade of the barn.

At the same time when I was just turning nine and we were coming to terms with the Santa Ana River rabbits, the town house I now live in was being built. Here on a quiet street in what's called the Avenues neighborhood of Chico, most of my neighbors are contracted with one of the pest control services available in town. Thus, their yards are periodically sprayed and mine isn't. I think that makes me especially attractive to pests who pretty much have the run of my yard without interference. Ants are a particular complaint of those who resort to pesticides. Ants can be a nuisance and, having put up no defenses, I've acquired a vigorous colony of resident ants to share the property with. In the spring and summer, they form a busy caravan that seems to emerge from the foundation of the house, crosses the lower step of the front porch, and continues along a planter curb to a spirea bush where they milk the aphids that occupy its limbs. "My" ants are aphid farmers, tending the aphids the way a dairyman tends his cows, protecting the aphids from predators and harvesting aphid honeydew. The ants are so organized and industrious in all they do that they seem to mirror an intelligent intent like that of my own mind. I don't like to interfere with their lives.

Yet I'd like to get rid of the aphids. They're sucking the life out of my spirea. But if I get rid of the aphids, I'll break the whole economy of the ant colony. Besides, if I watched the aphids with the same curiosity with which I watch the ants, I probably wouldn't want to interfere with them either. Perhaps none of us are so different in nature from E.O. Wilson and Bert Holldobler, who spent a lifetime observing the lives of ants and who in the end could attest to the remarkable social organization found there. If we took the time to look at the life of any creature, we might not be so casual about putting it to death. So I step carefully over the ant caravan where it crosses the front steps, and I find ways to discourage them without harm when they get into the house. I feel a little foolish sometimes putting up with all of this while my neighbors on all sides live in sanitized, insect-free environments. Visitors are often quick to point out that I have ants running over my porch steps and are more than a little perplexed when I ask them to be careful not to step on them. When I'm tempted to call in somebody to get rid of the ants, I recall that old quarrel with a population of hungry rabbits years ago. Remembering then how it was resolved, I end up leaving the ants alone.

BY RIGHT OF MERCY

*I hold to the image of a young boy who long ago
cradled an injured swan in his lap.*

ONE WHO FOLLOWS the Buddhist path walks in the footsteps of the life and teachings of the Buddha. Awakening, as I have described it, is taught by all the genuine masters, ancient and contemporary, as the realization of your own true nature. You can't awaken something that isn't already present. So it is that several events in the story of the Buddha's childhood foretell the presence of the awakened compassion that accompanied his eventual enlightenment under the Bodhi tree.

A tale of the Buddha's inherent sympathetic response to the natural world is told in an event that occurred when he was still the young prince Siddhartha residing in his father's kingdom. Edwin Arnold in his verse biography of the Buddha, *The Light of Asia*, tells that the young Siddhartha was out in the royal garden on a spring day with his cousin Devadatta who had with him a bow and arrow and was intent on finding something to hunt. When a flock of wild swans passed over on their way to their nesting grounds in the

Himalayas, Devadatta shot down the lead bird. Here is how the downing of the swan is told in Arnold's moving lines of verse:

> And Devadatta, cousin of the Prince,
> Pointed his bow, and loosed a willful shaft
> Which found the wide wing of the foremost swan
> Broad-spread to glide upon the free blue road,
> So that it fell, the bitter arrow fixed,
> Bright scarlet blood-gouts staining the pure plumes.

Seeing the fallen swan struggling to regain flight, Siddhartha ran to the swan and took the bird

> Tenderly up, rested it in his lap—
> Sitting with knees crossed, as Lord Buddha sits—
> And, soothing with a touch the wild thing's fright. . . .

And when Siddhartha had calmed the swan, he pulled the arrow from its wounded wing, and

> Yet all so little knew the boy of pain
> That curiously into his wrist he pressed
> The arrow's barb, and winced to feel its sting,
> and turned with tears to soothe the bird again.

When Siddhartha's cousin Devadatta demanded that the bird be turned over to him, arguing that it belonged to he who shot it down, Siddhartha refused to release the injured bird. But Devadatta argued that the swan was rightfully his because "'Twas no man's in the clouds, but fallen 'tis mine." Siddhartha responded to Devadatta's claim acknowledging that were the bird dead it might well belong to Devadatta, but since "the swan lives," it belongs to he who preserves life. Acting from the native wisdom of a young Buddha's compassionate heart, Siddhartha

> Laid the swan's neck beside his own smooth cheek
> And gravely spake, "Say no! the bird is mine,
> The first of myriad things which shall be mine
> By right of mercy and love's lordliness."

At Devadatta's insistence the issue was taken before a council of elders to judge to whom the bird belonged. At length the elders spoke:

> "If life be aught, the savior of a life
> Owns more the living thing than he can own
> Who sought to slay—the slayer spoils and wastes,
> The cherisher sustains, give him the bird."

The council's judgment of the dispute was remarkably consistent with the present-day views held by the proponents of deep ecology. Life, the elders were saying, *is* "aught," *is* the ultimate standard for judging the right and wrong of the matter at hand, *is* the reliable measurement whereby justice is best served. And the elders further insisted that life rests in the hands of those who preserve it. The young prince Siddhartha had taken the stricken bird into the refuge of his wide and accommodating heart. The elders in their wisdom saw that any claim to the bird rightfully resided in such mercy and love.

And we, all of us, must learn to see that it is by this selfsame right of mercy and love that the myriad things of earth are held in our keeping. While the story of Siddhartha and the swan reads like a simple child's tale, it nonetheless by its very simplicity stamps itself on the heart. Am I not the one who bends the bow and lets loose the arrow? The one who stricken falls to earth? And most of all, am I not the savior of life who comes to rescue? If I do not do so, who will? If it is not *my* love and mercy that mends the torn wing, whose then?

I have said that you can only awaken something that's already present, that the sight of the stricken swan called forth from Siddhartha what must already reside within him. But what then can be said about Devadatta who brought down the swan and now wants to claim the right to finish the kill? Why hasn't compassion for the creature arisen in him as well? If we humans can only give rise to what's already present within us, how do we account for Devadatta's lust to kill? Was there no compassion present in him to arise? Robert Frost, who was once poet laureate, noted that iron ore can be fashioned into either tools or weapons. And then, in a little rhymed couplet, described our human circumstance this way:

> Nature in her inmost self divides,
> To trouble men with having to take sides.

It follows that we humans bear within us an innate capacity for cruelty and indifference as well as one for loving-kindness and sympathy. We are at once both potentially sublime and utterly mean, a circumstance that forces us to choose. Devadatta wasn't a mean kid. He was just on a hunt, an apparent activity of his culture. He was doing what he was taught and encouraged to do. I'm not mean either, but when I was myself a boy I once shot a rabbit in much the same way that Devadatta shot the swan. Some local farmers and others from the state Fish and Game Agency were called out to exterminate a population of jackrabbits that were feeding on the immature pods of a nearby lima bean field.

To tell the truth I didn't like guns much and didn't want to join the hunting party. But my brother, Rowland, who was a hunter and whom I desperately wanted to please in those days, kept after me to go. We all lined up in a row and proceeded through an orange grove to flush out the rabbits that took shelter in the grove during daylight hours. And then there it was, a young jack bursting out from beneath the branches of an orange tree and racing ahead of me with its long ears flattened back. In a flash, I'd aimed and shot. I watched the rabbit jerk about on the ground, quiver, and go limp. Later, Rowland was proud to tell the others that I was one of the few who'd scored a hit on the hunt. I'd won a brother's approval and forfeited my own.

Perhaps many if not most readers have never been on a literal hunt. But consider the "hunts" you have been on. Consider those occasions when you were intent on doing one thing or another, and how being attached to a particular activity served to set aside doubts about what you were doing. Behaviors that are culturally instituted are especially potent in fostering this sort of ethical blind spot. In our single-minded pursuit of wealth and power, we wound earth itself, cursed by a universally ingrained habit in which whole nations fight over what dwindling resources the earth has yet to offer. And we do so without suffering the attendant remorse one might expect. In this manner, we have come to the place where we threaten not only the remnant populations of swans that have managed to survive among us but every other living thing as well, including ourselves.

But the Buddha in his compassion has given us the foundations of mindfulness that we might bring to awareness the consequences of our actions. Knowing that we humans are capable of both good and harm, he has put in our hands the very tools most needed to choose the good. When I feel the Devadatta in me reaching unwisely for something I want or claiming my right to something that's not rightfully mine, I hold to the image of a young boy who long ago cradled an injured swan in his lap. I trust that the compassionate heart of Prince Siddhartha is my heart as well and that I can call upon it now when loving-kindness is so sorely needed.

BUDDHIST ECONOMICS

It was a great satisfaction to know that we could
feed ourselves on what others throw away.

I'VE NEVER BEEN much of a consumer, rarely purchasing
something I didn't actually need. I can't credit my own relative
restraint in this matter, because I've never earned more than a
modest salary. I don't know what I might have done had I had the
money to do it with. What I can say is that I've never really wanted
a lot of things that others find indispensable. I learned the value of
thrift early in life, having grown up on a small family farm during the
depression years of the thirties and the years of rationing during
World War II. As a youth I didn't have to cope with the endless
enticements to purchase that today's youngsters deal with. Credit
cards were unheard of and people worked fulltime just to supply
the essentials.

Nearly all my family owned was visible from the back porch: a
kitchen garden with a few fruit trees, a milk cow, a half dozen pigs,
and some chickens running about the yard were the sole source of
our living. We were fortunate to have this much, and thought very
little of what we didn't have, perhaps because what we didn't have

was mostly out of reach. I don't ever remember feeling deprived, and I don't consider that impression as simply a child's naïve view of things. I honestly recall that we were perfectly content with what little we had.

Why do I now indulge memories of a period of United States history occurring over sixty years ago? I do so because it was a time when an industrialized nation of considerable wealth was forced to curtail its consumption of material goods, discovering in the process that a pleasing and agreeable life was consistent with such constraints. Now as an adult, I've adopted a Buddhist economic heritage characterized by modesty and restraint. It's an economy that distinguishes between "need" and "want." The needs of any one person, household, or township are finite, while wants are without limit. Wants reside in the mind, a product of thought, while needs are of the body, consisting of such reasonable necessities as food, clothing, shelter, and medicine. A simple analogy makes the distinction more tangible: wanting to eat is eating when you feel like eating; needing to eat is eating when you're hungry. It's a distinction upon which the survival of earth's delicately balanced ecosystem relies.

In a little mountain valley at the foot of California's Mt. Shasta lies Shasta Abbey, a Soto Zen monastery. To enter the Abbey is to enter an economic refuge where the standard of living isn't measured by the capacity to consume, where needs are distinguished from wants, and an unspoken moratorium on unnecessary consumption is in effect. Working one day in the Abbey kitchen, I was given a crate of lettuce to make ready for inclusion in a salad. It was discarded lettuce thrown out by a market in the nearby village of Mt. Shasta as too far gone for public sale. It was pitiful, a wilted mess that I couldn't imagine anyone would be asked to eat. But the monk in charge of the kitchen patiently explained to me how to tear away a few of the more blemished outside leaves of the lettuce and put the rest to soak in a large tub to rehydrate. When the lettuce had soaked awhile, I was surprised to see how revived it appeared to be. The leaves had filled out and begun to look like something I might not mind eating. With a few other greens, tomatoes, grated carrot, and parsley from the Abbey garden added, we all sat in the dining hall and ate a perfectly delicious summer salad. It was a great satisfaction to know that we could feed ourselves on what others throw away.

THE NATURE OF PLACE

*When we've lost our place we're like trans-
planted trees whose roots long for native soil. A
bond has been broken that can't easily be put
together again.*

ORANGE COUNTY is a place that happens to be located in
Southern California. But a place is more than a location.
Of course, if you know the convergence of a place's lati-
tude and longitude, you can pinpoint its exact position on the
planet. This will tell you where it's at, but not what it is. If you want
to know what a place is, you could start by recalling what it's like to
shut down your house when you're going away for a while. Shutting down your house is a little like untangling yourself from an
intricate web of relationships that you and the house have spun for
yourselves during the time you've spent together.

To begin with, there's the garden with the potted plants you've
been watering daily, the lawn you mow once a week, the sprinkler
system to be programmed and watched over, the bird feeder to
replenish, the leaves you rake, the flower beds you fertilize, the
shrubs and trees that require pruning as soon as the weather cools,
the vegetable plot with tomatoes and squash that are ripening and
need to be eaten. The garden and you are involved in an ongoing

dialogue of mutual understanding and the garden is just one element in the intimate relationship you have with the place where you live. Who will take your part in that relationship when you're gone? Who but you knows all the little moves that sustain the balance you and your place have achieved with each other? Who will be there to open up the windows overnight to cool the house down and close them in the morning to shut out the summer heat? Who will feed the cat and make sure it has fresh water and take it to the veterinarian if it comes home scarred from a fight? And not only that, but who will say hi to Mary across the street when she's out pruning her roses or backing the car out of the driveway to go shopping. And who will read the accumulating mail that's being held at the post office in your absence?

Shutting down a house reveals the nature of place as indistinguishable from its inhabitants; you and I are every bit as much a component of "place" as are the walls of the rooms we inhabit. That's obvious when you consider that a "room" is defined as such by virtue of housing occupants. That's what makes four walls a room, just as a chair is only a chair if it's to be sat on. So while a place is always somewhere and therefore has location, that location itself consists of a network of indivisible relationships without which place itself would cease to exist. A tree in a forest exists as an object in place, but its existence is inseparable from the hawks nesting in its branches should they happen to be there, and inseparable as well from the forest floor in which it takes root and the sky overhead and the sunlight dappling its leaves.

I came to better understand the significant nature of place in my life when places I cared for were lost to me. It's a loss that's particularly acute if you happen to lose a place where you spent your childhood years. And the effect of such a loss is pretty much the same whether the place was lost to fire or foreclosure or whether it was demolished to make way for "development," the latter being a means whereby whole neighborhoods are lost, with shopping malls and subdivisions substituting themselves for familiar neighborhoods you've known since you were a baby.

I know this loss firsthand. I was born and raised in Southern California's Orange County at a time when the entire county consisted of family farms along with a smattering of small towns whose high school graduating classes numbered fewer than a hundred graduates in any one year. If you went to school at Tustin, Orange, Costa Mesa, Newport, Santa Ana, or Garden Grove (as I did), virtually the only distinction to be noted between one school and another would be those of the school colors and which basketball or football team you cheered for. So while we had our differences, we were nonetheless a cohesive society and our cohesiveness resided in the land we shared. We all knew the intimate workings of the alfalfa, vegetable, and bean fields, the dairies and hog farms, the poultry farms, the walnut and orange orchards that spread across the county. These were the places where we lived out our lives. And just as our various farms bounded each other along fencerows and irrigation canals, so too did we sit comfortably side by side in the high school auditorium to watch the annual senior class play. We all had farms on our minds, and so wherever we happened to meet each other—either there in the school auditorium or the town hall or Schneider's Market or Ogden's Pharmacy or Alber's Feed Store—we met in a bond of mutual understanding known to us without explanation or prompting.

To have a farm on your mind is to be in dialogue with a piece of land. It's a conversation that's never finished because the circumstances of place continually change and what you need from the land and what the land needs from you is forever variable. When the dialogue is broken and the conversation terminated, the subsequent loss is irreversible. The irreversible loss of Orange County occurred when the living land was reduced to mere location. The fields we'd come to know by patient attention and respectful care, and upon which we depended not only for our livelihoods but for whatever community we held in common as well, these same fields were being newly calculated as simple acreages, a cost factor, a commodity for exploitation by corporate development.

In 1949, the year before I graduated from Garden Grove High, my algebra teacher, "Pop" Eidelson, sold his orange orchard to the Disney Corporation as a site for the proposed Disneyland. It was the beginning of the end of the Orange County that I or any of us who'd spent our lives there would ever be able to recognize as home. Pop Eidelson's orchard was one of the best, but from the time the sale closed escrow, the trees were never again watered, nor the field fertilized, nor any of the surviving fruit picked. As an orchard, Pop Eidelson's land was simply worth nothing to its new Disney Corporation owners, its entire value reduced to a space for eventual construction. The field was soon fenced off to prevent trespass, and from outside the enclosure we watched Pop Eidelson's trees wither and die, an occurrence emblematic of the pending fate of an entire county, whose contract with the living earth would soon be so undermined that nothing would be left of the age-old faith we'd once shared with each other and the land.

One by one the farms were sold to developers whose eagerness to cash in on the building boom elevated property values beyond anything farming could ever justify. And with property taxes based on market value rather than use, many families simply couldn't hold on to their own land. Not only that but the growth of agribusiness increasingly threatened the survival of family farmers who found themselves paying more to raise a crop than it could be sold for. Three years without a profit and further into debt, the Jensen family sold their farm to keep from losing it to their creditors. I was away at the time, drafted into the army and serving overseas. And by the time I'd married and worked my way through college with the aid of the GI Bill and taken up teaching at a Northern California college, nothing of the Orange County I once knew had survived the onslaught. The Jensen farm was buried under a shopping mall—the horse pasture, the garden, the fruit orchard, the grape arbor, the house and yard with its lawn, the sycamore trees and Chinese elms, all had disappeared under an asphalt parking lot. Shoppers were parking their cars on the very spot where the Jensen family once gathered round the table for evening meals.

All across the county you could find the newly displaced residents of Orange County, old farm couples who like my parents had taken the profits from the sale of their land and retired, living like refugees in one of the endless subdivisions that characterized the instant metropolis that had overwhelmed their lives. You could find them killing time at Harvey's Barber Shop or Natty's Tea House or one of the few original businesses that had survived the expansion and modernization of the county's towns. In Garden Grove, Alber's Feed Store was reduced to selling pet food and supplies, but a few of the old farmers could be found sitting on the loading platform, talking of hay and dairy feed and alfalfa prices as though such still existed. I knew it was more than land that was lost when I saw my father carting home a dozen ceramic squirrels to perch in the limbs of an ornamental olive tree that the subdivision landscape plan had allotted for the backyards of every one of its lots. This was a man who'd been coaxing life out of dirt since he was a boy in a farming village in Denmark, and now without any dirt to coax anything out of, the frame of mind that had sustained his bond with the living earth was reduced to this pathetic purchase of his at the Tustin Garden Shop.

There was at least one "hold out" that wouldn't sell. And perhaps better than anything else I might have witnessed, their plight measured the extent of the county's loss. Their names were Jim and Celia Warner, an old farming couple, who with the help of their eldest son George farmed a small acreage of vegetable crops. They lived on one of the county's original dirt roads in a yellow two-story farmhouse with double-hung windows trimmed in blue and a wide elevated front porch with steps leading up to the door. They'd once bought the place for something less than $8,000 and raised four children there, all of whom had married and moved away except George, who remained home and helped keep the farm going. When the neighboring farms joined into an agreement to sell to a development company that planned an extensive housing and shopping project for the site, the Warners refused to join with them and, since their property was essential to the developer's plans, their refusal pretty much ruined the deal for everyone else. Eventually the development company went ahead and closed the deal with the others, calculating that sooner or later the Warners would have to give in.

And they did to a degree, forced to sell off portions of their farm to pay the property taxes on what was left. In the end, they were left with only the house itself with its backyard garden and ancient weeping willow tree. Their house was at best a curiosity and at worst an eyesore to the county's new inhabitants. You could drive by and see the old relic with the backyard willow drooping like a flag of defeat, a shiny new Chevron station backed right up to the property line, the dirt road paved over and widened to four lanes, which, by the process of eminent domain, had sliced off the

Warner's front yard, leaving the porch steps descending directly onto the pavement. They died there—Jim Warner first, Celia soon after—in their $8,000 house with its little backyard garden, one of the last vestiges of original Orange County farm land. When the old house was eventually demolished to make way for a drive-thru Starbucks, I saw in its demise that it was not merely one more house and farm that was lost, but that the county itself was lost, all its distinctive character of place gone and the community of people who wrote out that character in deep affinity with the living earth gone as well. Those who were driven out of the county and those who stayed behind were both equally refugees, victims of "dis-place-ment."

When we've lost our place we're like transplanted trees whose roots long for native soil. A bond has been broken that can't easily be put together again. The once-living soil of Orange County now lies buried beneath sidewalks, streets, parking lots, and the foundations of endless buildings strung side by side from the mountains to the sea. For those of us who've known the county's farms and fields, a return to the county is like a visit to a vast graveyard where earth itself has been entombed. "Out of sight, out of mind," an old saying goes. And so for Orange County's current residents, the land that lies beneath their very feet is out of mind. When something is out of mind, it's not likely to be valued, and if what happens to be out of mind is the earth upon which our own continued existence depends, we're in trouble. "Orange Counties" of whatever name they happen to be called have sprung up across the whole expanse of our nation, and generations of youngsters are growing up with no more intimate exchange with the earth than is accorded by an annual pilgrimage to a National Park. For these young ones the ancient dialogue with the land has been effectively broken.

Like so many others of my generation, I've witnessed the place of my birth, indeed the world of my birth, erased like incidental words from a blackboard never to be rewritten again. I fear what this loss of place portends for each of us, humans and otherwise. Will we lose the wisdom that earth itself teaches? We need to go home again, and we need to remember that our real home is the very dirt under our feet. It was a footing we were once intimate with.

WHEN TOO MANY ARE NOT ENOUGH

In an important way, enlightenment is simply being present in whatever one happens to be doing at the moment.

WHILE LIFE in a modern industrial nation such as ours is increasingly characterized by complexity and multiplicity, we inwardly long for simplicity and singleness. Give me one instead of many. Give me just this moment instead of a host of worrisome hours to fret about.

Complexity is a persistent characteristic of the modern collective mind perpetuated by its own momentum. It's a habit that adds "more" to "more" and ultimately threatens the sanity and balance of earthly life. The material nature of actual things and events may very well be complex, yet it's a complexity that's best approached by taking up one detail at a time. It's like attending a buffet dinner where the sideboard is set out with more good things to eat than one could ever manage to find space for on a single plate. Perplexed by the sheer multiplicity of alternatives, I'm torn between the obvious limits of appetite and the fear of losing out on something good. It's a situation where too much is not enough. Realizing that I'm one person, with one plate, and one normal appetite, I could simplify matters by setting aside other alternatives for the moment, and picking out one item that appeals to my immediate appetite and starting with that. The abiding principle of simplicity resides in the realization that every "bite" you or I will ever take is a singular chewing and swallowing not to be weighed against the merits of other possible mouthfuls either actual or hypothetical.

Yet we humans find ourselves possessed of an untoward economic response wherein a plethora of alternatives feeds the craving for more. It's a puzzling contradiction I've witnessed in animal behavior as well. A pelagic crab is a tiny red crab that resembles a miniature lobster and drifts on the open ocean feeding on plankton. Every six to ten years warm ocean currents will distribute these crabs as far north as the California coast where they are an apparent novelty to the sea gulls and pelicans that inhabit these waters. I've seen these crabs turn the inland waters of California's Monterey Bay into an immense red carpet undulating up and down with the incoming swells. Confronted with this limitless feast, sea birds, accustomed to searching far out to sea for food, simply go crazy with the plenitude of it all. There are simply too many crabs. They end up gorging themselves in an unceasing feeding frenzy that continues hour after hour for days on end. Everywhere you look, the rocky cliffs and outcroppings, the wharf, the anchored boats, lampposts, parked cars, the sidewalks adjacent to the shore are stained red with bird excrement.

Brown pelicans feed by diving headfirst into the water while scooping their prey into their open bills. They typically feed on herring-like fish, and for a California brown pelican, a bay full of pelagic crabs is an unprecedented circumstance. They don't know what to do when availability so spectacularly outstrips need. I watched a raft of such pelicans floating on a thick mat of red crabs where all they had to do was open their mouths and scoop them in.

But knowing no other way to feed except by diving, they would from time to time pump their wings up and down, straining to lift their bodies so sodden and sluggish with ingested crab that it was all they could manage to get themselves fifty feet or so up into the air in order to plunge right back into the whole mess of crabs as though they were targeting an illusive herring.

When the pelagic crabs drift into shore, the whole population of Monterey Bay sea birds enact a perfect analogue to the apparently irresistible attraction that occasions the potent and addictive allure of encountering limitless options. You can witness a duplicate behavior almost any day at virtually any shopping mall across the whole of our nation. We humans multiply the numbers and kinds of things we feed upon. We call this duplication of numbers "progress." But too much is too much. That's why reducing the number of alternatives is essential to simplifying life.

It appears axiomatic to me that to live well, I must live simply. Either I limit the pointless distractions that occupy time and mind or forfeit life as a consequence. Henry David Thoreau made this point in a chapter of his book *Walden*:

> I went to the woods because I wished to live deliberately, to front only the essential facts of life, and see if I could not learn what it had to teach, and not, when I came to die, discover that I had not lived.

Am I living my life when I'm taken up by the allure of numbers and novelty? Am I living my life when I can't rest in the quiet of my own rooms? And if I can't, have I ever really inhabited my own skin, or shown up for life at all? To live life authentically, Thoreau calls on us to simplify, warning that "life is frittered away by detail."

Reverend Dazui, a monk of the Order of Buddhist Contemplatives, encouraged the Buddhist practice of mindfulness as an antidote for a life frittered away by detail. Mindfulness as he taught it was essentially a matter of simplification. He called it "every-minute meditation" and it consisted of five steps, four of which I've repeated here:

1. Do one thing at a time.
2. Pay attention to what you are doing.
3. When your mind wanders to something else bring it back.
4. Repeat step number three a few hundred thousand times.

"That's all there is to it," Reverend Dazui explained. "It's incredibly simple and requires nothing more than the willingness to do it." The willingness to do it grows with the doing, because, until you've tried to simplify your life in this way, you can't really know how joyful it is to live in the present moment without the distraction of alternatives. Simplicity, as I am speaking of it here, is synonymous with clarity. If I do one thing at a time, my life will be clear and present. If I eat breakfast without catching the morning news broadcast or reading a newspaper or setting up appointments on my cell phone, I'm left to simply attend to breakfast, something I may not have done for a long time though I might very well have sat with the same bowl of oatmeal in front of me for the better part of a lifetime. The old Chinese masters sometimes distinguished between the enlightened and the unenlightened by saying that one who is enlightened sits when he sits, stands when he stands, walks when he walks, eats when he eats, and sleeps when he sleeps. In an important way, enlightenment is simply being present in whatever one happens to be doing at the moment.

The simplicity of doing one thing at a time and being present in what I'm doing allows me to understand what's right before my eyes. When I was a boy in Orange County, Hector Berrens horse-farmed eighty acres of lima beans on a farm next to our own. I would sometimes see him walking the rows of growing beans, stooping to touch a plant here and there, sometimes plucking a leaf to smell or bite into. Occasionally he'd take up a handful of dirt and sniff it or even at times taste it, letting it sift through his fingers back onto the ground. Watching him, I was curious about what Hector was doing and sometimes tagged along to see if I could figure it out. I couldn't have put it into words at the time but I came to realize that the texture and taste of a single leaf on one plant in an eighty-acre lima bean field told Hector more about the condition of the entire field than any generalized survey of the field as a whole would ever yield. Hector knew the value of simplification. He understood that a bean field is best known one plant at a time. He would never have guessed that he was practicing Buddhist mindfulness.

The restless human appetite for an endless multiplicity of available diversions robs us of our rightful lives and threatens the balance of human life on earth. I would rather, as with Thoreau, front the essential facts of life. If I wish to live deliberately as Thoreau once did at Walden Pond, if I wish to learn what the fields of my own life have to teach me, I must look into the particular field at hand; for until I take the time to truly see a thing in its own right, I won't know what life requires of me. When I turn the handle on the kitchen faucet to fill a basin with water, I may be unaware that I'm giving and receiving a message from earth. But that little twist of the wrist that sets the water running is no less intimate a communication than were I dipping water from a nearby creek. Simplify,

simplify. Watch the water flow from the faucet to the basin. All that's needed is to watch the water, and you'll see where you are and what's happening and what needs to be done.

A MATTER OF SCALE

*A Buddhist values the intimate and the small,
measuring time not in years and weeks and days
but in the moment at hand, measuring space
not in miles nor yards but in the step now taken.*

THE PROPER SCALE for human endeavor is that of the household. It's within the intimacy of a household that we first learn to interact with other people and it's in our own backyard that we learn to interact with earth. We move from the center outward, comprehending the large in terms of our knowledge of the small. If we evolve at all from members of a single household to members of a global household, we do so by preserving the qualities of the smaller context within the larger. Our capacity to accept and include others depends on this vital connection.

We humans lose our way when we disregard the small and think and act on a scale so large and comprehensive as to distance our thoughts and actions from the smaller details of which the larger scale is comprised. This matter of scale applies not only to social interaction but to our interaction with the earth as well. A household scale of exchange is the proper currency of small farm economies. A family farmer can walk the smaller acreage of his farm and so comes to know each acre in its particularity. Just as he responds to the varying needs of family and friends, so too does he respond to varying needs of each acre on his farm.

In contrast, if you're an "operating engineer"—as corporate farm tractor drivers are called these days—you may very well be tilling a patchwork of thousands of acres that stretch out for miles. In which case you're likely to be sitting eight to ten feet above ground in the air-conditioned, sound-proofed, comfort-suspended cab of a model 9630 John Deere tractor with its 540 horsepower engine rolling forward on four gigantic sets of dual wheels, eight wheels in all, at speeds of up to fifteen miles per hour. And your primary occupation will not be with details of the field far below but with the computerized Command Center monitor that keeps the tractor in line, controls the overlap of its passes and programs the turn-around at the borders of the field.

Except for what the monitor readout tells him, an operator occupying an insulated cab at that height and at that speed knows nothing firsthand of the field below. He is prevented from doing so by the scale of his undertaking. For him, small scale distinctions are necessarily disregarded. And it is by virtue of this disregard that the corporate farming practices of the developed world are so damaging to soil, water, and air.

A Buddhist would not honor nor lend himself to a system of farming that brings harm to the living earth, produces food unlikely to sustain good health, deprives the defenseless poor of a traditional source of living, and replaces the value of human labor with the indignity of monitoring a computer screen. A Buddhist values the intimate and the small, measuring time not in years and weeks and days but in the moment at hand, measuring space not in miles nor yards but in the step now taken. He would know that to live his life he must do so here and now, an ancient and simple wisdom that accords with the inherent nature of earth's ecosystem.

This matter of scale affects not only the way we relate to domestic uses of earth but how we relate to wild places as well. While a statistical overview of a natural ecosystem can provide a valuable quantitative assessment of its condition, it's the intimate encounter with the details of an ecosystem that spells out its qualitative values. It's one thing to read that the burrowing owl population in California's Central Valley has been on the decline for the past fifty years, but it's quite another thing to watch the construction of Chico's South Mall bury acres of burrowing owl habitat under a layer of concrete and asphalt. If like Richard Redmond, you'd actually gone out to the site season after season and set up a spotting scope to watch the owls; if you'd seen them emerge from their burrows with broods of newly-hatched chicks trailing behind; if like Richard you'd watched them standing as high on their twiggy little legs as a burrowing owl can, their bright yellow eyes scanning the field for any danger that might happen to be about; if you'd seen them herd the little chicks back into the burrow when the shadow of a predator passed over the field; if like Richard Redmond you'd seen these things firsthand, you might know—as no one who hasn't seen these things can ever know—what it really means to lose another population of burrowing owls to urban development. It's a matter of seeing things exactly as they are, keeping faith with reality. Like Richard Redmond, I want to walk the field for myself, see for myself what the terrain is really like. It's a practice that teaches me how inseparable I am from my surroundings, how intimate are my connections to others.

Scale, as I've come to understand it, is an experience of size, number, and distance. How large or small, in how many numbers, and how near or far from my point of perspective is the event under consideration? If even a distant event occurring over large spaces in great numbers is viewed from the scale of a household, it can be understood in its intimate detail and a human perspective can be brought to bear upon such large scale events such as those of world hunger or wetlands destruction or the loss of wildlife habitat or the inches of annual topsoil lost or the extent of global deforestation. If I want to understand what recent worldwide temperature increases actually mean, I might try investigating it from the viewpoint of those Indonesians whose island communities are sinking beneath a rising sea.

I love the long sweep of a landscape—the great grass prairies of the Dakotas, a lowering sun illuminating miles of mountain peaks spread along the crest of California's Sierra Nevada Range, a stretch of Pacific Ocean beach with wind-blown waves rolling in from the far horizon. To my eyes, a span of great space, number, and distance is beautiful, but a handful of beach sand taken up, a tuft of prairie grass pulled, the slick feel of glaciated granite on a mountaintop help me to *understand* what I'm seeing. "Each branch of coral holds up the moon," Master Baling Haojian tells us. Whether taken figuratively or literally, the moon is big, and a branch of coral is small. Still, each branch of coral holds up the moon, just as each handful of soil holds up the field, and just as the field itself and the row of cabbages, the hawk resting on the fence post, the wheelbarrow by the barn, and the clothes hung out to dry, each in turn hold up the whole vast ecosystem we call earth. The large and small enact an ageless dialogue of seamless exchange. The scale of the universe is realized in the household, and we humans are asked to cultivate the larger field of life one shovelful at a time.

DIGGING HOLES

*Nature has its own wisdom, an inherent har-
mony born of natural consequence.*

ONE REVOLUTIONARY INSIGHT consequent of the Buddha's enlightenment is that there's no such thing as a
single occurrence, any event being an event at large. He
saw the extent to which the whole of the psycho/physical world is
linked together as one mutually responsive organism. Not only that
but the responsiveness, as the Buddha realized, is not sequential
(one event *causing* another in time) but simultaneous (a reciprocal
engagement of one event *with* another). The Buddha clearly saw
that this reciprocal responsiveness is the nature of the world we live
in, and his most direct statement of that is found in his teaching of
the *paticca samuppada* or "dependent co-arising" as the Pali term
is often translated to mean in English.

The Buddha's teaching of the dependent co-arising is given in
both a longer analysis of a chain of interdependent events, typically
twelve in number, and in a briefer formulation that is easier to grasp
in its entirety:

This being, that becomes.
From the arising of this, that arises.
This not being, that becomes not.
From the ceasing of this, that ceases.

What's clear from this formulation is that "this" and "that" are linked in mutual responsiveness, not so much as a matter of one causing another but as a matter of mutual adjustment to one another—the instant one element moves the other moves with it because both elements are of one body. In a world of such seamless and simultaneous response, no possibility exists for an isolated act of any sort; any action taken in particular is an action taken in general. It's an insight that accords with a fundamental tenet of deep ecology: namely, that you can never do just one thing in nature. I can't so much as dig a hole in the ground without altering the nature of the landscape in which the hole is dug. So it might be good for me to watch where I dig holes and for what purpose and to what end.

To begin with, consider the fact that a shovelful of typical garden soil contains from billions to hundreds of billions of soil microorganisms. If I dig a hole of even modest diameter, I'm displacing an incalculable number of such organisms, exposing them to the ultraviolet rays of the sun, among other forces. A balanced soil is an active and vibrant environment. So when I'm out digging holes, I'm digging into a soil biota that houses not only microorganisms but earthworms, woodlice, beetles, centipedes, slugs, snails, ants, yeasts, bacteria, fungi, and protozoa, all of these playing an essential role in maintaining the soil's health.

And what about the shovel I'm digging with? How did that common garden tool end up in my hands? From what woods was the hickory gotten and in what shop was it fashioned into a handle?

Where was the ore mined and smelted and forged to make the blade? By what means of truck, train, or plane were these materials transported to various sites of manufacture and eventually to the hardware store where I bought the shovel to bring home? And by what expenditure of energy resources was this transportation powered? And for that matter, what resources are expended to power the legs and back and arms of the body with which I dig the hole?

Far from being a singular action, the hole I'm digging in the backyard is an action of the entire universe, requiring a revolving planet, sunlight, water, an atmosphere with oxygen and carbon dioxide, an earth comprised of soil and stored metals. Every action you or I take in nature is like that, a movement in an intricate web of interrelationships reaching backward into the past and forward into the future. It is for that reason that we can never do just one thing in nature.

It's not necessarily a bad thing to dig a hole, or for that matter to plow up an entire field or plant a crop of potatoes or harvest hickory wood for handles. The problem comes when we don't consider what else is happening.

Recently, Butte County in northern California where I live recorded an increasing occurrence of West Nile Virus in humans from which a few infected individuals have died of a severe neurological disorder associated with the virus. And so the Butte County Mosquito Abatement District began spraying with pyrethroids to kill off the mosquitoes, driving through residential neighborhoods with a truck releasing a pyrethroid fog and flying over wetlands and agricultural fields spraying from overhead.

The intention was to save human life, which at first glance seems like a reasonable thing to do, except for the fact that the pyrethroid spray isn't specific to the mosquito vector but kills off every other insect it reaches as well. After a mosquito abatement truck fogged the street I live on, the crickets grew silent and remained so for several months. Not only that but mosquito predators like the dragonfly are killed off along with the mosquitoes. Much worse, and more threatening in the long run than West Nile Virus is to human life, is the fact that you can't kill mosquitoes by means of insecticides without killing the essential pollinating insects upon which we rely for many of our foods. And further unintended consequences of the spraying with insecticides are seen in the reduction of insect-eating birds who are themselves mosquito predators and the sickening of humans who are inadvertently exposed to insecticides and whose numbers far exceed the numbers of West Nile Virus cases reported nationwide.

Here in Butte County, we set out to get rid of the mosquitoes and ended up exposing people to an increased risk of breast cancer in women, lowered sperm counts in men, incidents of severe respiratory disorders, and irreversible nerve damage.

There's an old saying that exhorts one to "keep your eye squarely on the target," a practice that's reputed to be a good thing. In dealing with the earth's ecosystem and our place within that system, such a single-minded focus isn't necessarily such a good thing. It's much better to keep your eye on whatever's around the target as well so as to consider peripheral consequences.

Along with the fact that we never do just one thing in nature is the fact that we never get rid of anything. I might like to think that I throw things away, but "away" is always somewhere. If I'm digging a hole, what do I do with the dirt I'm piling up? In that sense, I can't really "consume" anything either; I just pass it along downstream in one form or another. Both consuming and discarding are acts of redistribution that may very well change the structure and characteristics of something but that never cause anything to be used up or to go away. It's good for me to keep this in mind when I set out the trash for North Valley Disposal or pile up leaves and clippings for the city to cart away or purchase something (anything!) at one of the area stores. Nothing that can be bought and carted home is ever taken out of circulation. If I buy packaged or bottled goods of any sort, every scrap of packaging or plastic or glass is either reused, recycled, or ends up in the landfill. If it gets burned, it ends up as ash and greenhouse gases. Even the food you and I "consume" eventually goes downstream and has to be dealt with if we are to avoid poisoning ourselves with our own excrement.

I understand now that any intervention I make into the ecosystem will reverberate throughout the universe. And I know that my actions can be either helpful or damaging. Nature has its own wisdom, an inherent harmony born of natural consequence. If I can act in accord with that harmony, I can shape my actions to earth's own economy and thereby avoid introducing harmful consequences. It's good to notice where the dirt is piling up.

WHAT'S FAIR

*Our human livelihood is held in mutual trust
with all other beings, the survival of the earthly
community predicated on an unavoidable prerequisite of fairness.*

WHEN I KNEW for a certainty that the Buddhist Way was
my life's Way, I was given the four bodhisattva vows, the
first of which is "Though beings are numberless, I vow
to save them all." "All beings?" I asked. "People, birds, trees,
stones?" "All beings," I was told. "How," I asked, "do I save all
beings?" "By letting them in," I was told. Though I didn't quite
grasp the implications of it at the time, in taking the vow to save all
beings, I'd committed myself not only to "save" my family, friends,
the checkout clerk at the grocery store, and supposed enemies, but
sticks, stones, dirt, forests, and rivers as well. I'd undertaken a practice of total inclusion.

It turns out that the science of ecology also emphasizes the inclusion of all beings. And it does so by citing the primacy of *relationships* between objects in an ecosystem rather than the primacy of the
discrete objects themselves, focusing on process rather than entity.
Human thought occurs in a format of language, which, in its capacity to name things, draws attention to nouns and noun clusters,

whereas ecology reveals a world of verbs in which the status of an ecosystem resides in the relational properties and exchanges of all its components. Humans and human civilization is one of those components. And so are mountains and rivers. The view taken of an ecosystem by the ecological sciences supports the ageless wisdom expressed in the bodhisattva vow to save all beings by including them. Together they argue a radical environmental as well as social ethic.

Social ethics refers to human society and how it is organized, the way people behave in groups and interact. But how we humans behave toward each other can't be separated from how we behave toward earth itself. It's not very useful to think of social and environmental ethics as separate disciplines. A simple consideration of social justice, for example, of how people share resources, should make it apparent that social and environmental justice are inextricably linked. I find it useful to think of justice and injustice as a matter of what's fair and unfair in human exchange. "Fair," with its origin in Old English, seems to better suggest the living qualities and behaviors of sharing resources than does the more abstract Latinate term "justice."

We are already consuming beyond the earth's capacity to provide, and the cost of such willful indifference and greed, if not acknowledged and corrected, will be paid for by the eventual collapse of human society and perhaps even the earth's ecosystem. Our human livelihood is held in mutual trust with all other beings, the survival of the earthly community predicated on an unavoidable prerequisite of fairness.

Despite the scope and prevalence of unfair behavior, equity ultimately prevails. And it does so as a matter of conscience and subsequent regret. All appearances to the contrary, we humans are host to an inherent sense of fairness that when neglected or denied reasserts itself of its own accord. If you or I cheat or finagle others out of things that are rightfully theirs, we subject ourselves to a regret that regardless of the degree of our denial works its way into our hearts. Regret is an ethical corrective, an agent of what Buddhists call *karma*. Regret is a medicine offered a sick heart as a means of healing itself. It can be a bitter remedy, but I'm grateful for the healing it brings, however painful that may at times be.

Fairness calls upon us to share the earth equally with its many beings in an attitude of mutual interest wherein no distinction is drawn between self and other. The Buddha identified a source of suffering in the failure to share. Suffering, the Buddha taught, is an inevitable consequence of the human predilection toward chasing after things. When my outlook is shrunk to the scale of personal greed, my place in the world shrinks to the same meager scale. It is then that I call upon the force and intention of the vow I have taken to save the many beings. What I ask of that vow is to pry open the clenched fist of greed, and let fall from my grasp whatever I've managed to get hold of.

Give me an empty hand.

Let there be whole nations of emptied hands, innocent of grasping and holding, capable at last of passing along whatever is given.

RINGING THE BELL

If I just carelessly slap at the bell, I'll get a careless ring and will continue to do so until I ring the bell carefully.

I WAS ONCE TOLD of an exchange between a Zen teacher and student. The teacher was conducting *dokusan* interviews (encounters for face-to-face Zen teaching) and the student had come to him with a question. As was customary, the student rang the bell before entering the dokusan room, and the teacher told me that, unlike her typical behavior, she just sort of slapped at the bell. "Her ring was awkward," was how the teacher described it to me. And when the student was seated before the teacher, she asked him, "How can I truly love?" That's a large question for anyone to ask, and the teacher's response was direct and to the point. "Be present when you ring the bell," he told her. The student bowed and left the room.

It seems me that the teacher had touched upon a quality essential to truly loving: that of giving all our attention to the details of our lives. Our capacity for loving depends upon our being fully present. And this mindful presence that's asked of us, while often experienced as an affectionate regard for our surroundings, is not so much a sentiment as it is an unreserved showing up in person for the occasion.

I don't know how it is for others, but when I'm fully present to the bell, the bell rings itself. It's a little like the bell and I are ringing together. I think earth gets rung in this way as well, the whole of earth being nothing but the bell ringing. And so the quality of attention essential to living on this earth is not a willed or forced concentration of any sort, not so much a matter of striking the bell correctly as it is a willingness to allow the strike to occur in its own time and by its own means.

We're not here on this earth to achieve ends. We're here to live, and we do so by allowing life to unfold of its own accord. In that way, the means of life are themselves their own ends, and by their unfolding we find the way to care for ourselves and earth, the way to love one another, the way to grow and to age, and eventually the way to die.

As a species, we have wrongfully subordinated means to the service of eventual ends, forgetting that means are themselves ends. It is exactly that error that accounts for much of the damage we inflict on earth and each other. If I just carelessly slap at the bell, I'll get a careless ring and will continue to do so until I ring the bell carefully. If I blow the tops off mountains in order to get at the wealth of coal lying underneath, I will by that means destroy mountains and pollute everything downstream. And this won't end until I quit blowing the tops off mountains. Dr. Martin Luther King Jr. pointed out this obvious yet often neglected truth. "The ends are preexistent in the means," he reminded us. It's clear to me that I'll never get a sweet ring out of something I'm just slapping at.

Understood rightly, "means" is simply a word for the way things work, for the inherent movement of life itself. Our lives, yours and mine, if allowed to do so, flow like an unimpaired stream that cycles from the high mountain snows to the valley rivers and out to the broad sea, only to rise again enacting its own return to the mountain, continuously reborn in its own doing. We're all invited to enter that stream. But when we refuse to acknowledge the water's own terms, when instead we project our own designs upon the current, we're likely to end up like a school of salmon stalled at the base of a dam we ourselves constructed with entirely different ends in mind. By our own inattention and misguided interference, we add ourselves along with countless others to the earth's growing list of threatened and endangered species.

We are a species obsessed with the prospect of accomplishment, looking past the present moment toward what we think we ought to be or ought to do at some future time. What we ought to be is what, deep down, we already are. What we ought to do follows from that fact, something the earth is forever showing us if only we would stop to notice. It's simple. Life with earth only requires that I be fully present in the relationship.

When I do that, the exchange rings true.

A LOOK INTO THE MIRROR

*It's an instance in which nature claims me as
her own.*

SPIRIT ROCK Meditation Center rests in a landscape of
grassy hills dotted with clusters of California live oaks.
Karen and I have come here to attend a retreat led by the
eco-philosopher Joanna Macy. At 10 a.m. under a sunny morning
sky, on the fourth day of the retreat, Joanna sends us out into this
landscape. Her instructions are simple and unremarkable. We're
each of us to pair up with a partner, one of whom will lead the other
who will be blindfolded. The one who is blindfolded is dependent
upon the leader to explore a sightless world of sound, smell, and
touch. The interesting variation Joanna introduces into this typical
blind walk is that from time to time, the blindfold will be lifted and
you'll be asked to "look into the mirror"—into nature itself.

People begin pairing up, and I'm holding back as I tend to, troubled not to impose myself on someone who might prefer another
partner. Apparently the number of us present is divisible by two
because when everyone else has picked a partner, there are two of
us left. My default partner is a woman in her midforties, slim with

quick eyes and dark hair swept back into a braid. "I'm Margaret," she says, and adds, "It looks like a case of the shy leading the shy." And while she might very well be shy, she isn't too shy to say so. Nor is she too shy to slip the blindfold over my eyes, apparently having determined that she'll lead first.

Blindfolded, I can't see more than the presence of light leaking through. Margaret has me by the arm leading me from the meditation hall and onto a path into the surrounding hills. I feel the uneven rise and fall of the earth beneath me and the warm brush of a breeze scented with the smell of ripening grasses. Then she has me kneeling to touch a small low-growing plant of some sort. I rub a leaf between my fingers and smell the sweet scent of mint. Without sight some of the most familiar objects seem puzzling. I run my hand along the horizontal length of some unaccountable object, like one reading Braille, until I realize that I have hold of a fence board, and, sure enough, feeling my way further along the length of it, I come to what is unmistakably a fence post. Having spent a quarter of my life on a farm, stock fences are as familiar to me as sidewalks to city-dwellers, but apparently I've never really known what the touch of a fence board exposed to seasons of wear actually feels like to the unsighted human hand. And so we go on, running my hands over the polished mass of a granite boulder warmed by the sun in a field of wind-blown grasses, the one so solid, the other dancing beneath my fingertips.

And then we're going downhill, dropping out of the warmth of the sunlight into a place of moist coolness, and when we stop, Margaret says, "Look into the mirror," and slips the blindfold from my eyes. I find myself looking into a fiercely brilliant cluster of orange and black-spotted hibernating ladybugs packed into a dense heap on the moss-covered trunk of an ancient live oak. At the moment, the ladybugs, the moss strewn arching limbs of the oak, and the grassy undercover take up my whole person. It's as if I had to go blind for a bit in order to see the obvious. It's an instance in which nature claims me as her own face and body. For the moment, I entrust myself like the cluster of hibernating ladybugs to the winter's sleep. I spread out toward the sky like the arching limbs of the ancient oak. A deep green moss clings to me like my own skin.

It's been a decade since my visit to Spirit Rock, yet my reflection still appears in trees and rocks, in clouds, in watercress lining the margins of the creek, in the heaps of beans and squash at Saturday's farmers' market. Of whatever forces and substances the life of the earth is comprised, the very same are the forces and substances that comprise my life as well. And what's more, the earth and my person are one indivisible life. Can I but keep this truth foremost in mind, I can better understand how best to live out my stay here on earth. I'm tied to the body of earth's being as I was once tied to the body of my human mother who cradled me and fed the cells of which I'm made even before I'd tasted air of my own. And while a human infant can have the umbilical cord cut between it and its mother and still survive on its own, the cord that ties me to the earth is never cut. I need to be mindful of that.

KITCHEN

In a kitchen, earth shows up to speak for itself.
For the cook the task at hand is to listen to what
earth has to say.

THE KITCHEN is one of the places where life drops out of the abstract and lands squarely onto the cutting board. Cabbages, squash, carrots, beets, eggplant, potatoes, mushrooms, and asparagus—if it's grown and can be eaten it shows up in the kitchen sooner or later. It's here under my fingertips that life itself gets sliced and chopped and grated, sautéed, simmered, steamed, boiled, roasted, broiled, and baked.

I like kitchen stories and one of the best of them comes from eighth-century China. The story goes that the monastery cook had a pot of rice cooking on the stove when Manjushri, the bodhisattva of great wisdom, rose up out of the pot and began to expound on the dharma. Of all the mythological figures in the Buddhist pantheon, Manjushri is perhaps the most treasured because he embodies the wisdom of ultimate enlightenment. So here the cook is with his pot of rice going while he's maybe chopping up vegetables or washing up the cookware or some such thing. And then in the midst of these seemingly mundane chores, he's suddenly blessed with the offering of a Dharma teaching from the very body of wisdom itself, the words of which are certain to be profoundly wise. So what does this monastery cook do? He grabs a hefty cooking spoon and whacks away at Manjushri, driving Manjushri along with all his priceless wisdom back into the cooking pot. Then he slams the lid down tight so that the bodhisattva can't get back out again.

Since first hearing this story, I've run into several variant interpretations of its meaning. But from the start, the story was without any "meaning" for me at all other than "Don't bother me while I'm cooking." In a kitchen, earth shows up to speak for itself. For the cook the task at hand is to listen to what earth has to say. There's no need to have Manjushri about to interpret for you. If I'm cooking potatoes, it's the potato that tells me about potatoes. A potato tells me that it's good baked, roasted, fried, boiled, and steamed but that it's not so good eaten raw. A potato by its own nature ends up in soups and stews, mashed and smothered in gravy, baked and garnished with salt, pepper, sour cream, and chives, fried into hash browns and served with eggs. It's not the cook, but the potato itself that chooses the company of leeks, carrots, red peppers, roast beef, and hamburger.

Recipes are a record of the lessons cooks have gleaned from their conversations with food. A cookbook is earth's own scripture, a dialogue of communion with the land, a consequence of generations of exchange with the earth. A recipe gives testimony to this exchange, pointing the way for others engaged in the ongoing conversation. I like to bake bread. And when I lived in the mountains, far from any source of good bakery bread, I baked quantities of it. One concern, of course, in baking bread is to get it to rise properly. And toward this end, I'd been taught to knead the bread thoroughly. Nothing less than an all-out effort could assure that a properly risen loaf would eventually emerge from the oven.

Yet, all the while that I was baking bread in my remote mountain valley, Edward Espe Brown was baking bread at Tassajara Mountain Zen Center in the Ventana Wilderness inland from Big Sur on the California coast. There, in his encounter with flour, yeast, oil, and water, Ed Brown discovered something that only the bread itself could teach. Ed was always an experimenter, and so rather than stick with what he'd always done, he tried something new. It was simple really. Instead of adding all the flour to the water at one time and then kneading the subsequent lump of dough into some semblance of elasticity, he mixed only half the flour into the water, whipped it with a spoon about a hundred times and set it to rise. And rise it did, quickly swelling to the very rim of the mixing bowl. From then on, there was no more concern about getting the bread to rise, but rather one of containing the rise long enough to get the rest of the flour mixed in and separated into loaves to bake. When I tried Ed Brown's bread recipe for myself, the dough was literally swelling under my hands as though it were of its very nature to rise.

In his book *Tassajara Cooking*, Ed Brown has this to say about cooking:

Cooking is not a mystery.
The more heart we put out
the more heart we put in.
To bring cooking alive
we give our life.

I too have learned that cooking is not a mystery if I simply give myself to it. In the kitchen, everything is just what it is and in plain sight. Life for Ed Brown, whether in the kitchen or elsewhere, is a simple and direct matter of putting our heart out in order to put our heart in. In doing this, we give our lives. This, he tells us is our freedom, our wisdom. It just so happens that for me the kitchen—with its pots and pans, mixing bowls and utensils, the counter strewn with cabbage or corn, a clump of kale or a heap of green beans, a pot full of brown rice set over a low flame, a crock pot of potato, onion, rutabaga, carrot, and grass-fed beef growing tender over the slow hours of a winter afternoon—is one of the best places to give my life. There in midst of all this kitchen wealth, with a soiled apron tied round my waist, a hot pad in one hand, a whisk in the other, stirring milk and cheese into a thickening pot of polenta, I carry on my dialogue with earth.

I give my life to the earth's life; earth gives its life to me.

A GATHERING OF SPIRIT
LIKE RAINWATER

*I think there is nothing but spirit. It's the very
stuff of matter itself, the source of that deeply felt
connection with living earth.*

I WAS ONCE asked if there was such a thing as spirit. It's a question worth consideration.

Spirit is difficult to talk about or even think about because talking and thinking are conducted in the medium of language, and language has no exact vocabulary for matters of spirit. If I want to identify a valley oak tree, I can say the words "valley oak" and the words have an actual concrete referent that can be pointed to. I could take you to a valley oak and show you the very species of tree that the words name. But what can I show you as a referent for a word like "spirit"?

Perhaps we humans look for spirit in unusual or rare experiences because ordinary objects and events don't seem good enough to qualify. Poet Mary Oliver teases us with the notion that perhaps the ordinary might be special enough. "The spirit," she reminds us, "likes to dress up like this, ten fingers, ten toes."

Like anyone else, I experience certain events as more significant, memorable, or even more transforming than others. It's not that a sighting of midnight geese tracking their way across the face of an autumn moon is no different than, say, peeling potatoes. It's just that in terms of spirituality one is not more or less spiritual than the other. When I think something is more spiritual than something else, this is only an arbitrary persuasion of the mind. Is spirit really less manifest in sweeping the floor or washing the dishes than in offering a prayer or sitting an hour's silent meditation?

I was given an insight into how spirit manifests itself in ordinary matters one night while walking home from a lecture at the university. I was engaged in thoughts about the topic of the lecture and my agreements and disagreements with what had been said. The sky had cleared after a recent rain and the stars were bright above the bare limbs of the winter trees. Then I noticed the reflections of the stars gathered there in puddles formed on the pavement. The puddles glittered like tiny duplicate heavens. The pavement was literally suffused with starlight as were the sidewalks that lined the avenue, the yards and houses of my neighbors, my ten fingers and toes.

I'd been living in a star world all along, and it took a puddle in the street to show me that. I don't know what to name an occasion like that; but there it was, a gathering of spirit like rainwater. The stars overhead and the stars cast in puddles on the pavement were the body of the one star that animates the entire universe. As an ancient Buddha put it, "Each branch of coral holds up the moon."

The truth is I think there is nothing but spirit. It's the very stuff of matter itself, the source of that deeply felt connection with living earth that characterizes the Buddhist path. Spirit takes us up into its own body, which is the body of earth itself. It opens on an undivided presence that issues from the one intelligence that governs earthly reality. It tunes us to every atom of being, sentient and insentient. It thinks us and speaks us and does us, for we are nothing but spirit itself.

I'm a profound materialist just as spirit is profoundly materialist, though I'm not materialistic in the sense of needing to possess
things. I just like material. I'd just as soon hold in hand a clod of raw
earth or peel cabbage leaves or cleave a winter squash in half to bake
for an evening's meal than take up the wisest scripture written on
the subject of spirit. The squirrels that inhabit my neighborhood
know more of these matters than I do. All summer long, they dig
holes in my lawn to bury seeds and nuts they've gathered, where, in
the winter, they dig them up again to eat. Squirrels just naturally
know how to do spirit, or rather spirit knows how to do squirrels.
Better yet, spirit knows how to do spirit.

A Zen student of mine once taught me something about how
spirit does spirit, and how spirit is indistinguishable from the thing
it does. She came to tell me of a day when she was walking along
Chico Creek under a canopy of oaks and sycamores. She stopped
to rest on the bank of the creek where a sandbar formed a backwater and the water circled on itself. And then she said that for a
moment she didn't know whether she was the creek with its current
and backwater or the one on the bank who was watching the creek.
"Was that it?" she asked me. What she wanted to know was whether
or not her experience was one of enlightenment, or spiritual as she
put it. "It was what it was," I answered. She thought for a minute
and said, "Then I'll call it the day I traded places with Chico
Creek." "How many places were there to trade?" I asked. "Two,"
she said as though that were an obvious consequence of simply
counting the parties involved in the trade. But then, just as quickly,
she said, "No. One. There was one of us!" She understood that
Chico Creek with the current flowing by and the little backwater
stalled behind the sandbar and the girl on the bank watching were
each none other than this one spirit that pervades the whole universe and gathers us up with the body of earth.

Spirit is a condition of circumstance itself, indistinguishable from the configuration of the present moment. It is wisdom like that of the nucleic acid that contains the genetic instructions used in the development and functioning of all known living organisms. A tomato seed, of its own becoming, manifests its nature as a tomato plant and doesn't become a cabbage. The birth, growth, and maturation of any living thing including ourselves is surely a spiritual event, requiring the attendant wisdom of sunlight, air, water, and soil as midwives. Indeed, the very fact that I can draw breath depends upon a spirit infused with inherent wisdom born of an entire universe. Yet if knowing something means to wrap my mind around it in ways expressible in logic, language, or thought, then I don't know spirit. But spirit knows me. Spirit knows me in the way that the fetus developing in the uterus is known by its human mother and in the way that she in turn is known by the mother of us all.

I've said more about this matter than I know to say or have a right to say, and so I'd like to end these thoughts with a disclaimer. I'm really a simple man. There's so much I don't know. The Buddha taught that knowledge of any sort, no matter how "true" that knowledge might be, is useless unless one experiences it for him or herself. When I ask myself what truths I have actually verified, it becomes apparent how vast is the extent of things I don't know. And so I'm as inclined to seek guidance from a stone or leaf or paper clip as I am from the soundest advice I might give myself. I'm supported more by what I *don't* know than by what I know.

I can only trust that spirit's message is somehow getting through to me.

VICTORY GARDEN

The nature of the garden's "victory" was one of slow growth and a patient tending of living things.

D URING WORLD WAR II, my brother Rowland and I shared a single bed in the cramped upstairs bedroom of the Seventeenth Street farmhouse we Jensens called home at the time. On a shelf adjacent to the bed lay a few twisted fragments of metal from a downed P-38 fighter plane. I alone of all the family saw the plane go down. There were seven or eight fighter planes in the skies over Orange County practicing "dog fights" when two of them collided somehow in midair. I saw them come together and then separate, one of the planes pulling free and the other plummeting nose downward like a dropped bomb, its twin engines streaming a trail of smoke and fire. I watched as it disappeared beyond a row of eucalyptus trees, my body taut with the expectation of the great explosion I expected. But there was no explosion, just a heavy dull thump and a sensation like that of a wave rolling underfoot as though from an earthquake. Already in the distance the other planes were heading out over the sea, mere dots now on the far horizon. With their departure, an odd stillness settled over the farm as though nothing had happened.

I got to the site before anyone else, and stood on the cavity of a great hole like that of a bomb crater. The plane had disappeared into its own gravesite with only a few fragments of twisted metal from the fuselage strewn about on the churned up earth to testify to its presence. I'd seen the bodies of the dead lowered into graves and covered with dirt before, but never anything like this. It was troubling to imagine the body of the pilot somewhere there below my feet. Had he just disappeared with the plane? Was he still in the cockpit? Would he be left where he was or dug up and buried in the town cemetery? I tried not to think of it.

Like all of us farm boys I seldom wore shoes in those days, going about my chores and even to school on feet toughened enough to run unprotected on gravel or a field of alfalfa stubble. And so I felt my way barefoot down into the crater, sinking ankle-deep into earth sifted like fine powder. An unnatural warmth oozed up from below. The dirt felt hot to my feet. In the bottom of the crater, I gathered up a few exposed scraps of the plane's fuselage, the largest of these no bigger than the length of my hand. When the sirens approached, I climbed back out and faded away into the surrounding orchard, not waiting to see what would happen when authorities arrived and a crowd gathered.

In the following weeks, I told no one in the family or at school about seeing the plane go down or that I'd gone anywhere near the crash site. The half dozen fragments from the downed plane lay in a shoebox in the back of the upstairs bedroom closet. I didn't speak of these either, though it was a rare moment when they weren't on my mind. I don't know why I kept all this to myself. It wasn't because I feared anyone's disapproval. It wasn't even as if I were keeping it a secret. It's just that I didn't know myself what to say about any of this. Images of the crash played on in my mind's eye, and I didn't know what to do with the thoughts I was left with. It was a little like the time when Mother's foster father died, Grandpa Goslee, and Mother cried at the funeral and later again in the farmhouse kitchen. She didn't seem to know what to say either. And seeing her cry, I started to cry myself and she told me to stop crying and sent me into the yard to play. But I didn't play. I sat on the porch steps, and later when Mother lay down on her bed and fell asleep, I crept in to look at her. Her eyelids were closed and the room itself hushed. No one came to disturb us and so I sat and watched her for a while, and it seemed to me that whatever either of us weren't saying was being said somehow.

And so in the weeks following the crash, I held unspoken a P-38 pilot's fall to his death. And though I might very well have been the only one in Orange County to possess any surviving relics of that fall, they remained secreted and untouched in back of a closet where I never took them out to look at them. This might have gone on indefinitely if Mother, straightening up the closet one day, hadn't come upon the fragments of fuselage herself. I was present at the time, and all she said was, "Oh, Linley?" Just that, "Oh, Linley?" in a voice that echoed my own child's regret for their sad presence there.

After that, I came out of hiding, if hiding was what I was doing. A narrow shelf ran along the bedroom wall on my side of the bed, the kind people use to display what I called knickknacks. I didn't have any knickknacks myself and so the shelf was littered with a dozen or so polished river stones I'd found and a few seashells I'd gathered on the sands at Laguna Beach west of the farm. I rearranged these to make space for the P-38 fragments, and when Father saw them he said, "You were there?" not waiting for me to confirm the fact since it was obvious I was there. My brother, Rowland, said nothing of the fragments, picking up a single twisted piece of the metal and then putting it back without comment. After that, the whole incident of the crash appeared to pass out of the thoughts of the others in the family, and the P-38 fragments drew no more interest than any of my other nondescript collectibles.

But I was troubled by the presence of the fragments there on the bedroom shelf. It was as if I'd invited the war itself to share the room and bed my brother and I occupied. I often lay sleepless far into the night disturbed by the presence of an intruder to whom I myself had allowed access. When I carried those twisted little fragments of P-38 fuselage home from the crash that day, I unwittingly carried World War II along with them, and now images of that war flickered across the mirror of my mind like a continuous rerun of the newsreels I'd seen at Saturday matinees in Garden Grove's Gem Theater depicting scenes of violence at places with names like Normandy, Iwo Jima, Guam, Bataan. My coming and going in and out of the bedroom was a little like returning to that dusty crater in the neighbor's orchard where another human being had unaccountably been swallowed up. I could still feel the odd warmth of the crater on the soles of my feet, and it was as if I were being swallowed up as well.

As near as I can remember, all of us there in the farm country of Southern California were patriotic and intent on winning the war. One expression of this patriotism was the nearly universal planting of a "victory garden." With so many men enlisted or drafted off the farms, farm yields were down and local grocery stores simply hadn't enough food for those left behind. So the mothers and kids who remained were asked to feed themselves, and if need be feed their neighbors who might live in town and have little tillable ground for a garden or were too old perhaps to maintain one. On a farm of thirty acres such as ours, it would be shameful to be without a victory garden.

At the same time, every possible hope, everything good that might ever happen, seemed to depend upon winning the war, this thing called victory. I don't know what I imagined victory to be exactly, but I associated it with the fragments of a downed P-38 plane and with the violence and death associated with the crash. So I didn't at first associate victory with the rows of beans, cabbage, corn, squash, potatoes, and greens in the garden below, though that very garden was called a "victory garden." But it so happened that the garden was clearly visible from the upstairs bedroom where the fragments of the P-38 lay at my elbow when I looked out on the garden below. In time, the sheer juxtaposition of these two influences in my life brought me to consider victory in a different light.

I worked in the garden a lot in those days of the war, coming home from school to pull weeds, or harvest green beans, or turn water into the rows so that the roots might take up moisture and grow. I would cultivate the ground around cabbage and tomato plants and spread manure from the horse stable and cow barn. I liked doing these things. It was a respite for the mind of a boy troubled by some scattered scraps of metal he'd introduced into his life.

The days I planted seeds were the best of all. I'd work the soil loose and run a little furrow along the length of a garden row. And then I'd take a packet of bean or beet seeds and spread them evenly along the furrow and cover them with earth and give them their first watering. There was nothing to do then but wait while the earth and seeds did their work. It was such a hopeful waiting, the little seedlings pushing their way up in a victory of a sort different than I'd previously acknowledged. The nature of the garden's "victory" was one of slow growth and the patient tending of living things. It stood in contrast to victory in war that I could only imagine as the death of the enemy. The garden was without enemies of any sort.

Something happened at that time that brought my idea of the enemy itself into doubt. All the time that the war was going on, our nearest neighbors were the Sasakis who happened to be Japanese and who farmed the acreage adjacent to our own. They had a boy my age, Iko, who rode the bus with me to Lincoln Elementary School and who came home as I did to farm chores. The Sasakis too kept a victory garden, and sometimes exchanged produce with us. And then one day, Iko didn't show up at the bus stop—or the next day or any day thereafter. The Sasakis were gone, and their farm was leased to the Berrens, a Belgian family who grew lima beans, and who restored the victory garden the Sasakis had maintained. No one seemed to talk about the Sasakis, and it took a while to pry the truth of the matter out of my parents. I learned that they had been taken away to an internment camp in the Nevada desert. That's honestly the first time that it dawned on me that the Sasakis were Japanese. Iko was my friend and I hated the Japanese. After all, the Japanese were the enemy and the war propaganda films at the Gem Theater had shown me what inhuman brutes the Japanese were.

But now I had two versions of "Japanese" to contend with, and my innocently acquired prejudice was undermined by the disclosure. Since I couldn't hate the Sasakis, I could no longer simply hate the Japanese. Iko who had so often shown up at the back door with a basket of cucumbers and corn was a real person, while the Japanese portrayed in war films were only images on a screen. Partially formulated questions were arising in my child's mind. Could victory come from something so simple and natural as offering baskets of food to each other? Would the offering itself be a victory? If we all tended gardens and shared what we grew with each other would we need to kill each other as well?

Six decades later, I reflect further on the meaning of a garden. A garden is a seedbed where peace is sowed. It teaches care and patience. It brings the mind and body into the natural rhythms of the earth. The earth is not at war with itself as we so often are with each other. As a boy in wartime, I watched the garden below my window occasion its own victory over the violence that characterized the world. The victory of the victory garden was not realized in its intended support of the war effort, but rather in the affectionate care we gave to it and to ourselves and each other. Tending a garden taught us that.

There came a day when I took the P-38 fragments from my bedroom shelf and carried them to the garden below. I'd initially thought to dispose of them in the trash bin behind the garden shed. But then, not knowing why I did so, I buried them, like seeds, there in the garden among the hopeful rows of living things.

THE WHOLE WORLD
IS KIN

*May each continue to deepen their love toward
each other and toward all living creatures that
walk, crawl, swim, slither, and fly, above,
below, and over the earth.*

IMAGINE what it would be like if all the people of the world and
all creatures and beings of any sort were wedded to one
another in mutual caring and respect:

I straight, take you gay and lesbian . . .
I Christian, take you Muslim . . .
I Buddhist, take you Jew . . .
I robin, take you sparrow . . .
I rabbit, take you fox . . .
I frog, take you salmon . . .
I stone, take you leaf . . .

We have come together for this marriage. May each continue
to deepen their love toward each other and toward all living
creatures that walk, crawl, swim, slither, and fly, above,
below, and over the earth. I hereby declare that we are one
family of one earth, 'till death do us part.

Seng-ts'an, the third Chinese Ancestor of Zen, taught that "the ultimate way is not difficult; just avoid picking and choosing." Seng-ts'an's ultimate way is the way of the interface of all beings—human, animal, mineral. Legislating the exclusion of lesbians and gays from society denies the reality of our shared humanity, much like those laws and public policies that that legislate the exclusion of birds, animals, and plants from their rightful habitats or allow for the exclusion of salmon from their spawning sites and thus deny our essential human interaction with the earth.

From the viewpoint of the contemporary deep ecologist or like-wise one who has entered the Buddhist path, this sort of selective exclusion simply doesn't make sense. To the Buddhist it is like rejecting the shape of one's own face; to the ecologist it's a pointless and tragic argument with reality. If Seng-ts'an's ultimate way is one of compassionate inclusion and love, then I don't get to pick and choose who gets to love and who doesn't. And since to love is to cherish and nurture life in all its forms, then nowhere in the whole of this wide earth do I get to choose what stays and what goes. Whatever I deny to others, I've already lost to myself.

If we humans treat each other badly so will we treat the earth. We have sought to shape conditions to our own liking, an ignorance and greed that rests on the same fatal flaw: the belief that we can possess the world on our own terms. If I walk the path of prefer-ence, I will be constantly at pains to rid the world of whatever offends me. If instead I come to realize that our lives and histories are shared, then the whole world is kin and I take my place at the table where the entire earthly family is invited to dine. Who then will be told to go hungry? Who will be left outside?

Whenever diversity is feared as a threat, we suffer. Could we but open our hearts to all our brothers and sisters, our fears would drop away and we would celebrate at last the treasure of a rich and varied earth.

Indeed, the earth itself invites us into the all-inclusive body of life. Our human lives are not separable from each other or from the lives of earth's other creatures.

EARTH FEAR

To befriend earth and know its sublimity, we
must enter it on its own terms.

I CAME UPON a man I judged to be somewhere in his midthirties walking in Chico's Bidwell Park. His jacket collar was raised against a stiff spring wind. He appeared tense, repeatedly looking up at the canopy of ancient oaks and sycamores where the limbs swayed and creaked in the force of the wind. "I don't like it in the park when it's windy," he told me. "Why is that?" I asked. "A limb could fall on me," he said. "It's unlikely," I told him. "Yes," he admitted, "but it could happen." "There are trees like these all over town," I said. "Right," he answered, "but those trees are planted. There are sidewalks and houses. They don't just grow wild." Having apparently talked himself further into his fear, he said, "I'm out of here," and, with that, turned toward the park entrance.

The man in the park registered an exaggerated symptom of what I call earth fear. It's a fear characterized by discomfort felt in the absence of the domesticated world. Houses with their mowed lawns flanked by sidewalks and paved streets lend a human order to things. And even out on the freeway, the fields laid out in geo-metrical patterns with their attendant barns, fencerows, and grain silos, the billboards and service centers that flank the highway, the signs that mark county lines and freeway off ramps, all signal a familiar and reassuring presence of human activity. The man in the park might feel more in control of his circumstances among such constructions.

Of course, not many of us would be driven out of the park by the morning wind, but still some degree of this particular fear of nature is not uncommon among contemporary human populations and has a long history within the annals of human behavior. If one can judge by literary and historical accounts, the early American colonists literally clung to the town for protection from the sur-rounding forests. That there were actual dangers present in the woods is true enough, but the fearful distrust of the wild that played itself out in the cultures of the early colonists was quite another thing. Among the Puritan and Calvinist colonies of New England, this distrust of the wild took on psychological, religious, and moral proportions. The forest was where the devil ran free, and if you chose to wander about in the woods without good reason, you risked accusation and expulsion from society. Some of the best expressions of this town-versus-forest frame of mind are found in fictional accounts like that of the description of forest revelers in Nathaniel Hawthorne's "Maypole of Merry Mount":

> Had a wanderer, bewildered in the melancholy forest, heard their mirth, and stolen a half-affrighted glance, he might have fancied them the crew of Comus, some already transformed to brutes, some midway between man and beast, and the others rioting in the flow of tipsy jollity that foreran the change. But a band of Puritans, who watched the scene,

invisible themselves, compared the masques to those devils and ruined souls with whom their superstition peopled the black wilderness.

Not trusting what we can't control, we humans still people the wilderness with our superstition. We're uneasy with the unrestrained behavior of Comus, in whatever contemporary form he might appear. Comus, the Greek god of festivity and night revels, represents anarchy and chaos, a force out of control, an unrestrained spirit, a god of excess. In the imagination of the early American colonists there existed a causal relationship between disorder and the vast forests surrounding their settlements.

These old superstitions may seem ridiculously remote from contemporary attitudes toward the wild. But all one has to do is recall the lingering presence among us of the rather common fear of the dark, an often irrational fear that both children and adults sometimes experience. Remember when Dad had to turn on the light and show you that there was nothing hiding in the closet? That we still have our many ways of whistling in the dark is a legacy handed down to us from centuries of cultural distrust of those regions that lie beyond our capacity to control. The symmetry and pattern of a suburban subdivision with its grid work of streets and spaced lighting bears the stamp of human order and logic in a way that unaltered nature does not. And some among us, like the man in the park, aren't comfortable with that.

Mightn't we instead befriend nature? Among the literary tales of those who've made friends with earth, I like to include the biblical tale of Jesus' forty days in the wilderness. As the story goes, there on his long fast with only the beasts for company, he suffered the devil's attempts to turn him away from the life's work he'd set out to do. And when, in disgrace, the devil was defeated and left, angels we are told came to Jesus' aid. Had Jesus not chanced his encounter with the wilderness, what angels then would have come to him? His solitary stay in the company of the wild had purchased for him a message from heaven. John Muir on one of his wilderness trips into the high Sierra Nevada Range, once climbed to the very top of a great tree and clung there to ride out a wind-lashed rainstorm just for the sheer glorious misery of it. Thoreau, writing of his solitary stay at Walden Pond, wrote that he intended "to drive life into a corner, and reduce it to its lowest terms, and, if it proved to be mean, why then get the whole and genuine meanness of it and publish its meanness to the world; or it were sublime, to know it by experience, and be able to give a true account of it in my next excursion." What's apparent to me is that the angels sometimes come in great sheets of freezing rain or in a whole and genuine meanness. To befriend earth and know its sublimity, we must enter it on its own terms.

Whatever fears of the wild we humans might happen to feel, these fears are nonetheless trustworthy guides to places where we most need to enter. I know of no other cure for such earth fear than that of making its acquaintance, to do as Thoreau suggested and "drive life into a corner" and see for yourself what it's made of.

A MOST RIGHTEOUS HORSE

Coming to terms with a horse gives an intimate insight into how nature works.

THE ONE we're after is down in the flat where the sycamores grow, a horned Hereford brood cow with a calf at her side, grazing with a dozen other cows and assorted calves. Frank, the ranch foreman, pushes the quarter horse he's riding into a trot, and I follow alongside on Faline, a morgan mare I was given the day she was born. And now Faline and I are here on a summer's loan from the Jensen home farm to the Wheeler Ranch, a cattle outfit inland from San Juan Capistrano in Southern California. I'm sixteen years old, and that cow in the flat below is something I've prepared for since the day Faline was turned over to me by my father.

Though we horse farmed and kept a few saddle horses, the Jensen farm raised turkeys, not cattle. But I was always enchanted with the thought of cattle ranching, holding I suppose an unrealistic romantic view of what cattle ranching was actually like. By the time I was eight years old, I'd asked for a subscription to *Western Livestock*

Journal, and when my parents agreed to it, I cherished every issue, reading them from cover to cover. So naturally, when I was given Faline to raise and train on my own, what I wanted to make of her was a roping horse.

Father, a fine horseman himself, placed one nonnegotiable condition upon my training of Faline. I was not to put a saddle on her until I could show him that I had her under control without this aid. If you're sitting a horse bareback, you have to earn the horse's permission to ride. That, I'm certain, was Father's intent. So long before Faline was of a size and age to be ridden I was doing everything I could to accustom her to my presence—walking her about with a halter and lead rope, draping my arms over her back, swinging a lariat in her presence, lifting her hooves each in turn, and brushing her down regularly. When she was finally old enough to ride, I slid myself onto her back, feeling that we already had an agreement pretty well worked out. Her response was to buck me off, and it turned out that her attitude regarding this was a long time changing.

Coming to terms with a horse gives an intimate insight into how nature works. Faline had to learn to trust me astride her back. I had to learn to trust her instinct to throw me off, knowing somehow that the same persistent determination in her to toss me on the ground would someday serve to make a roping horse of her.

A roping horse has more to do than just run faster than a fleeing cow. It has to anticipate all the twists and turns, stops and starts, a cow might make in its effort to evade capture. And it has to do this mostly on its own because in the heat of a chase there's no time for more than the rider's knee pressure to signal to the horse what move to make next. To succeed, Faline and I would have to become a team of one.

Our first chance to try ourselves out as a roping team came unexpectedly. We always kept a milk cow on the farm, and Father was raising a replacement for the current milk cow, a soft brown Jersey heifer that was just getting to the age to be bred and brought into milk production. The Jersey had the run of the pasture for the time being and was always out among the horses that grazed there. But one day she showed up missing. The pasture gate had been inadvertently left open, and while the horses had stayed, the Jersey hadn't. We called all the neighboring farms and none had seen a loose Jersey cow, except Mr. Warren who thought he might have seen her on the Santa Ana River levee. By this unlikely means, the chance I'd been waiting for had at last come. I saddled Faline, hung a halter and lead along with the lariat from the horn. "Don't go lassoing her," Father said. "She's not a range cow. Just talk her into the halter. She's practically a pet." Of course I was itching to try out what Faline and I had been practicing for months but I knew Father was right.

Out on the river levee, I didn't see her for a long time and was just about to conclude that Mr. Warren had probably seen something else when she emerged through the willows from the river bottom. But when I rode toward her, she took off from us, trotting down the levee. It's the horse I thought. But when I left Faline at a stand and approached her on foot, she still fled. Back in the saddle, I shook out the lariat and began to close the distance between us and the cow, and the closer we got to her the faster she went until she was in a full-out run. It was then I felt Faline take over. She had the sense of chase in her and she closed on that brown Jersey in a matter of seconds. And when the cow suddenly cut down a steep side path toward the river bed, Faline was right on her and I let the lariat sail out and watched it close neatly over her head and horns.

Together, Faline and I brought the Jersey back to the farm on a halter and lead and Father never asked how we got hold of her.

Here now on the Wheeler Ranch alongside Frank, Faline and I aren't after a tame little Jersey weighing 800 to 1,000 pounds, we're after a Hereford that's been running wild since the day it was born and with a weight twice that of a Jersey. And as we close in and cows are scattering in all directions, Faline keys on the one we're after and Frank calls to me to let the horse go. And before I know it I'm in position and watch the lariat settle over the Hereford's big horns. Frank has the rear legs roped and the Quarter Horse and Morgan stretch the Hereford between them. Frank checks the Hereford's eyes and inoculates her. We call the horses in to let the lines slacken, and I slip the lariat from off the big cow in time to see her rise, shake herself, and trot off with her calf.

A dozen cows later and back at the Wheeler Ranch, we water the horses, feed them a bucket of oats, and brush them down. Frank watches Faline where I've released her into the pasture. She drops her muzzle to the ground and bites off a mouthful of grass. Frank says, "A righteous horse you got there, son." Righteous? I'm not sure I know what righteous means. Something religious? Something god approves of? I look to see what Frank is talking about. And what I see is Faline biting off shoots of young rye. That's when I know that if Faline is righteous, then so are Frank and me and the Herefords I've been chasing all day and their calves and the sycamore trees down in the flat and the little brown Jersey back home and the lingering taste of grass in my mouth.

SCAVENGERS

*It hadn't occurred to me that these scavengers of
trashcans, combing the back alleys and sidewalks of my hometown, were performing a public service.*

THEY COME in all ages and circumstances, from one like
Molly pushing a rusting shopping cart with all her belong-
ings in it down Main Street, who tells me she turned
ninety-one this year to others like the couple so young they might
be high school sweethearts except that the young father has a pre-
schooler in tow and the mother is hauling an infant suspended in a
baby sling. Molly, though homeless, considers herself a resident of
the town and makes her "home" here. The young couple tell me
they're just traveling through, trying to get the fare for a bus ticket
to Seattle. Do I have any spare change, a dollar or two? They don't
consider themselves homeless though they have no place to sleep
the night other than a riverbank or the underside of a bridge or at
best a cot at Torres Homeless Shelter. They're just on the road,
they say.

And then there are others: the veteran on crutches with a leg
missing, a painfully thin woman who walks around the downtown
streets talking heatedly to someone not visible to others, a half

dozen regulars who show up daily in the town plaza with their dogs and blanket rolls seeking shelter under the bandstand canopy when it rains. What all these street dwellers have in common is that they scavenge from trash and garbage cans whatever they can find of even the least value—a discarded wedge of pizza that's still edible, a cigarette butt with enough tobacco left for a few inhales, an aluminum can worth four or five cents at Safeway.

It hadn't occurred to me that these scavengers of trashcans, combing the back alleys and sidewalks of my hometown, were performing a public service. It took Billy Soder to show me that. When I first saw Billy, he was dragging an oversized load of recyclables on his way to the Mangrove Avenue Safeway. I intercepted him on a side street that wound its way through the Chico cemetery, linking Mangrove to East Washington Avenue. He was hitched like an overloaded draft animal to two shopping carts and a wagon he'd strung together to carry a load of cans, bottles, and plastic. Billy was in front straining against a heavy rope slung over his shoulders, the stack of recyclables creaking along behind him. The load looked so top heavy that I expected it to topple at any moment. The Safeway was still six blocks away, and I estimated Billy's progress to be about a couple hundred yards an hour at best.

I came along just as Billy stopped to take a breather and we sat down on the curb and talked. When I commented that, considering size of the load he was hauling, it looked like he was making a career out of salvaging recyclables, he agreed. "It *is* a career," he said, "except that I don't work for a company or corporation. I'm self-employed." "You make a living this way?" I asked. "I do," he said, "enough to get by. I can pay for what little I need." It turned out that Billy knew exactly what he was doing and why, and that he was marvelously articulate in expressing it. He held the philosophy that the work he did to salvage other people's wastes was an honorable and essential occupation in a throwaway society like ours; and when he got going on the subject, he laid the whole rationale out for me in detail. He was a man acting on deepest conviction. "I don't pull stuff out of the recycling bins," he told me. "Some do, but I don't. Everything you see on this load had been tossed into a trashcan and would have ended up in the Neal Road landfill. And I don't just go for aluminum like so many do; I take glass and all sorts of metal cans and cardboard as well. I try not to leave anything behind that can be recycled." The way that Billy looked at it, he was performing an essential public service and he was quite clear about the nature and value of that service. "The work I do helps to save the environment and makes up for some of the wasteful disregard of others," he explained. "I find things that are still usable. I do for others what a lot of people won't do for themselves. Reduce, reuse, recycle. That means don't buy it if you don't need it, and, if you do buy it and no longer have any use for it, pass it on to someone else to use, and if that's not possible, recycle. I dig into the trashcans of people every-day who can't be bothered with any of this and just throw things away."

Billy seemed satisfied that he'd said what was needed then, and we sat quietly for a bit. When he got up to harness himself back to his load of recyclables, he said, "You see these shoes?" pointing to those he was wearing. "Got them from a trashcan just last week. Do they look like trash to you? Can you see anything wrong with them? It just so happens that they're my size or I would have dropped them off at the thrift shop. Try to imagine who might have thrown a perfectly good pair of shoes like these away and what he might have been thinking while doing it. Personally I *can't* imagine what he was thinking. Perhaps he wasn't thinking at all. I don't know. Maybe it's that little puzzle of human behavior that keeps me doing what I'm doing."

The last I saw of Billy, he'd just passed through the cemetery gate onto Mangrove Avenue. I never ran into Billy again, but just a week ago I saw one of his colleagues digging into a trashcan on Broadway in downtown Chico. He was so thin and urgent in his search that he looked to me like the human counterpart of a stray and starving dog. He found a few things to eat and stowed them in a paper bag he was carrying. And then he pulled up an aluminum Coors can, a good find for him I thought. But instead of pocketing the can, he dropped it into the recycling bin alongside the trashcan. In doing so, he'd restored a little order and sanity to life on the streets.

If it weren't for Billy and the dozens of others who are dipping in and out of our trashcans, who would there be to sift through and salvage what we throw away? When I see these scavengers at work, I'm ashamed to just toss something out that I no longer want. I'm forced to pick up after myself.

OH, BEAUTIFUL

*If we cannot sing the earth's song, we cannot
sing our own.*

THE WORDS and music of "America the Beautiful" play in
the minds of most Americans like old friends and are as
familiar to them as are the names and voices of their own
family members. Many of us can recite the poem's first stanza from
memory.

> O beautiful for spacious skies,
> For amber waves of grain,
> For purple mountain majesties
> Above the fruited plain.
> America! America!
> God shed His grace on thee,
> And crown thy good with brotherhood
> From sea to shining sea.

For many of us, this verse, with its skies, fields, mountains, and
plains, its vaulting sense of space, names for us the America we call

home. The poem, sung or recited, is above all a celebration of the land's beauty.

Katherine Lee Bates, the author of "America the Beautiful," was a professor of English at Wellesley College when she was called upon in the summer of 1893 to lecture at Colorado College in Colorado Springs. The journey to Colorado was geographically like that of the nation's earlier westward migration, taking Bates from her familiar New England landscape on the Atlantic coast to the great Rocky Mountains of the American West. It was on that journey that she would have literally seen the spacious skies, the amber waves of grain, the purple mountains, the fruited plains. It's told that in Colorado, Bates joined with a group to climb the 14,000 foot-high Pike's Peak. So it could be said that Pike's Peak authored "America the Beautiful," for there on the crown of the mountain, Katherine Lee Bates was so inspired by the vast landscape she saw spread out about her that she took out a notebook and wrote the entire poem right there on the spot. Her muse for such a poem was that of the earth itself, as it is for us as well. If we cannot sing the earth's song, we cannot sing our own. If the earth's voice does not rise in our throats when we sing of our lives, our song will be thin and colorless and go unheard.

If Bates were to journey to Colorado now rather than in 1893, what would she see along the way and be inspired to write? Would she write of the beauty of freeway interchanges, the strip malls with their McDonalds, Burger Kings, and KFC franchises, the service centers with their gas pumps and convenience stores stocked with candy bars, chips, and Cokes? Would she write of the beauty of the litter strewn along the pavements of America? Would she be inspired by her overnight stays in motels so repeatable as to be indistinguishable in memory one from another? These questions are real and not meant to be merely rhetorical, calling for a resounding "No!" Perhaps Bates would espy beneath and within the tarnish of modernization and waste an underlying America whose deeper beauty survives and awaits its own return.

And yet, what makes of us one people and bonds us each to the other is the shared perception of the beauty of the land. Katherine Lee Bates understood this and gave us an image of an America graced with a brotherhood that spans the continent "from sea to shining sea." Whatever else might make of us a national family, it is surely a view like that from the crown of Pike's Peak, the spreading vista of earth below, the "Oh Beautiful!" of America, that turns us toward each other as true brothers and sisters of the land.

FRUITS OF REFUSE

*One of Erin's favorite mushrooms featured as a
centerpiece an old moss-covered shoe punctuated
with foxtails.*

HER NAME is Erin Wade, and she has an eye that can discern the presence of beauty in the most unlikely places
and forms. I first heard of Erin when an article concerning an art project of hers appeared in a weekly edition of the *Chico
News and Review*. Erin, I learned, had joined in an annual community cleanup sponsored by the Butte County Environmental Council. The difference between Erin and other volunteers that day was
that Erin wanted the trash for an art project. She had won a small
grant from the city of Chico and had gotten a permit from the Parks
Commission to set up a sculptural installation in Chico's Bidwell
Park made entirely out of litter. I first saw the results when Karen
came home from her morning walk and told me that the sculptures
were in place.

What I saw when I got to the site challenged my sense of aesthetics, asking of me to see beauty in something I'd always considered
ugly. Erin had set up her project on the moist lawn beneath the
spreading limbs of valley oak trees. The sculptures "grew" in the

shape of mushrooms, because that's what she thought might naturally occur there in the damp pockets under the trees. "Mushrooms," she reasoned, "heal the soil." And there they were, mushrooms spread out over the lawn and constructed of paper, discarded socks, bent cans, and chips of broken bottles, looking as if trash itself had taken on new life and recycled itself into living matter. One of Erin's favorite mushrooms featured as a centerpiece an old moss-covered shoe punctuated with foxtails. The *Chico News and Review* quoted Erin as saying, "If there is a major change in the way we live due to the state of the economy, or war, or global warming, how will artists make art? What materials will I use to make art after the apocalypse?" She wasn't entirely kidding in her prediction, and then she added, "I don't want to buy [new art] materials of any kind. It just makes sense to work with what you've got."

What we've already got is the beauty of the land and hopefully the will to restore that beauty wherever it has been compromised by wasteful neglect and indifference. Erin herself said, "Litter is ugly." She just wanted to take the worst of the ugliness and shape it into an expression of beauty, a reminder to all of us of what we stand to lose. She called what she'd done the "Fruits of Refuse," inviting all who passed that way in the park to take a second look at what they'd discarded.

WHEN YOU DON'T KNOW WHO YOU ARE

*It occurs to me that the who of "Who am I?"
might not be the best interrogative pronoun for
the inquiry and that "Where am I?" might serve
better.*

IT HAPPENS, and when it does it can be distressful. If I ask
"Who am I" and no reassuring answer is forthcoming, I can
feel as if my likeness ought to be posted in public buildings
along with other notices of missing persons. "Have you seen this
person?" the caption reads. When I don't know who I am, others
may perceive me as no different than I ever was but I no longer see
myself in familiar terms and so appear a stranger in my own eyes. I
don't quite know what to make of myself or how to fit into my life
anymore.

All sorts of occurrences can bring us to doubt who we are.
Maybe I lose a job I've come to identify with. Maybe my wife asks
for a divorce and I find myself living alone in some rented room
after years of sharing a house with a family. Maybe I become ill after
years of good health. Maybe I inherit a lot of money when I'm
accustomed to counting the pennies in order to get by. Maybe I
retire and find myself out on the lake dangling a fishing line into the
water, wondering what now? Maybe someone takes a photo of me

and when I look at it, the likeness that's printed there, the image that meets my eyes, is just too old to be who I am. Sometimes, without our ever knowing why, familiar identity just drains out of us like water wrung from a cloth.

Doubts of these sorts are particularly unsettling when they jeopardize some belief, faith, ideology, or philosophy that's been held on to for years. I'm a Zen Buddhist and see Zen as central to my identity, but it occurs to me that had culturally formative conditions been other than they were I might just as readily have been a Christian, Jew, or Muslim. I don't mean to suggest that there's no conscious selection involved in choosing a religion but only to point out that choices themselves are made within a culture of limiting circumstances. What if my being a Buddhist is merely conditional and arbitrary in nature? A look into that mirror raises all sorts of doubt. Well I *have* looked into that particular mirror, with the result that I can no longer say "I'm a Buddhist" with the same innocent conviction I once held.

I don't necessarily think I have more doubts than most, but I've never been good at adopting a belief of any sort. And this includes a belief in any consistent version of who I am. I once told a Rinzai Zen teacher of mine that I was distressed to discover that I not only didn't know whether I was a Buddhist or not, but that I didn't really know who I was at all. He congratulated me. Apparently it's not so bad an outcome to lose the person you thought you were.

There's a widely known exchange between the Emperor Wu of China and Bodhidharma, an Indian Buddhist who traveled to China and is credited as the first ancestor of Zen. The emperor asked, "I have endowed Buddhist temples and authorized ordinations—what is my merit?" Bodhidharma said, "No merit at all." The emperor then asked, "What is the holiest principle of Buddhism?" Bodhidharma said, "Nothing holy in it." Unable at this point to establish a criteria for identity with Bodhidharma and probably feeling a little loss of identity himself, the emperor asked, "Who are you facing me?" only to hear Bodhidharma say, "I don't know." The "person" the emperor was trying to identify in cultural and philosophical terms is simply an idea of self that for Bodhidharma no longer applied. He was never the person that the emperor was seeking, nor any other person he or anyone else might imagine. Bodhidharma's "I don't know" gave the emperor an opening through which to see that there was no one to be found except the one standing on his own two feet facing him. "I am just this whom you see, Emperor."

It occurs to me that the *who* of "Who am I?" might not be the best interrogative pronoun for the inquiry and that "Where am I?" might serve better. The *who* of "Who am I?" has in mind a generalization of a person with his or her attendant characteristics of temperament, talent, reputation, belief, activity, failure, and success, the whole biography. "*Where* am I?" on the other hand, has in mind an identity grounded in a specific place and activity without dragging in all the rest. If where I happen to be is bicycling to Saturday's farmers' market, then I'm just that person pushing the pedals round.

Despite the Buddhist insistence that "we walk on the empty sky," my feet have to meet the ground somewhere. And when I notice where that is, I'm no longer at a loss for self. Where I am *is* who I am. And where I am is on planet earth. I'm just he who's chaining his bicycle to the rack in front of Chico Natural Foods or I'm just he who's giving a lecture on Buddhist ethics to Religious Studies students at Chico State University.

I've never been attracted or comforted by encouragements to practice otherworldliness, whether I was promised in return a ticket to heaven as in theistic traditions or a favorable rebirth as in classical Buddhism. Whatever other worlds there might be, this world is where I am, and that fact alone establishes who I am. Identity is momentary to exact place and circumstance. Where I am is all I need to know about myself, all else falls in accord with that simple reality. It's my presence on earth that grants me being, and when death comes to take me from myself, it's earth that gives sanctuary to what remains.

MILKING THE COW

*Milking a cow is very much an in-the-moment
kind of thing, not an activity you can generalize on.*

WHEN YOU milk a cow by hand and not by machine, you
have to come to terms with the cow, which turns out to
be a teaching in how we humans must proceed if we
hope to live in harmony with the earth. You might suppose that
when you know how to milk one cow, you know how to milk any
cow. But that's not so; cows are individuals and each cow has to be
learned anew. Cows don't repeat themselves or come in duplicates,
nor does anything else on earth.

The Buddhist metaphor of one moon reflected in many waters
is sometimes interpreted to mean that there is one repeatable constant that runs through all nature. But the reflected moon never
actually repeats itself; it is rather taken up and modified by whatever object or being is host to its reflection—the host, reflection,
and all, manifesting solely as itself. In the same manner, there are no
two cows alike. In fact, there's no one cow alike either. There's no
singular source that manifests as "cowness," there's just individual
cows themselves.

Thus, milking a cow is very much an in-the-moment kind of thing, not an activity you can generalize on. It's the nature of earthly life to unfold like that. Even a cow that you've been milking for months on end, while familiar to you in many ways, can't be dealt with by rote. She herself has changes in mood and behavior. She's never quite the individual she was the day before. When you go out to the barn in the early dawn with a milking stool and pail, you need to meet her anew on that day's particular terms. In that way milking is no different than anything else we do on this earth.

I was probably about eight when Father turned over the morning milking chores to me—one milking in the morning before school and once again in the evening before supper. Father liked Jerseys, a relatively small cow, typically gentle, and one that gave good rich milk. Suki was our Jersey and I have no idea how she got that name, but by whatever name she gave enough milk, cream, and butter for the five of us in the family.

Father transmitted the dharma of cow-milking to me as clearly as it can be given as explicit instruction. Secure Suki in the stanchion with a quarter pail of oats and some dry hay to feed on. Wash her teats with warm, soapy water. Dry them, but don't rub them so hard as to irritate them. Place the milk bucket under the udder and take a seat on the stool. Lubricate your hands with Vaseline to keep down friction and wrap them around the nearest two of the four teats. Squeeze the base of one of the teats, and pull down gently to push out the milk. Don't force. Alternate one hand at a time. Continue this until the udder on the side being milked is soft and deflated. Then move to the other two teats.

The mechanics of milking were perfectly straightforward and I had no problem understanding what to do. Father demonstrated each point as he explained it, and it all seemed simple enough. And when Father had me sit in on the stool in his place for a few minutes, I squeezed on Suki's teats and watched in pleasure and satisfaction as warm milk flowed into the pail and a bright foam danced on the surface.

It turned out that the mechanics of milking and milking itself were two different things, because the next morning, in the pre-dawn hours of a cold November day, things went quite differently. In the dark stall, I squeezed and stroked and tugged at Suki's teats but only a pittance of milk droplets dribbled into the pail. I could feel her udder tight with milk, but she wouldn't let it down. I got confused as to what to do and reached for the other pair of teats but with the same outcome. All the time I was struggling in this way, she kept switching at me with a tail that lashed across the back of my neck as if I were a pesky fly to be rid of. She seemed distrustful of being milked by what to her must have been a stranger. She kept twisting her head around in the stanchion to get a look at me. In the near darkness, I could make out her large dark eyes under their long lashes peering at me. And then, when I'd managed to gather a bit of milk, Suki lifted a hoof and planted it squarely in the pail. Mother seemed forgiving of me and dumped the soiled milk into a barrel where we were soaking grain for the hogs. She fed me breakfast and sent me out to catch the school bus.

That evening after school, I went out to the barn with nothing but misgivings. I went through all the preliminary steps and sat myself down on the stool. Suki's udder was visibly swollen now with excess milk. I reached in under her and took a pair of teats in hand. They felt shriveled as though none of the milk had reached them, and I knew it would be useless to try to squeeze anything from them. Father was off at work with the Edison Company and wouldn't be home for another hour. Mother was in the kitchen waiting for the milk. I was an eight-year-old with an important job to do and no way to do it. I sat with her unresponsive teats in hand and felt like crying. "Oh, Suki!" I called out in despair, and in doing so I slumped forward on the stool, which left the flat of my face pressed against her broad flank. Instantly, I felt the warm rush of milk descend into her teats. That was it! Suki liked the feel of me pressing on her side. As in any intimate exchange on earth, only Suki could show me that.

A cow's flank is a warm and comfortable support to lean against when you're milking. People who milk cows must have known this for centuries. Perhaps anyone who's ever milked a cow comes in time to lean against its side. I don't know anyone who's ever taught that as a technique. You can go online these days and find detailed instructions on milking a cow, but none of these ever includes leaning against the cow as one of its recommendations. Perhaps it's too intimate for that or just something that Suki likes but that any other cow might be wholly indifferent to. Perhaps it's something one must discover for himself like discovering that your cat likes its ears scratched but not its back. Suki and I both like it when I press the flat of my face against her. When I do that, she lets down milk with a contentment like that of a cat purring. I like it because it's comforting on a cold morning and because I can hear sounds coming from inside her.

At length, the relationship between the two of us was like that of practiced old couples who know how to fit their lives together without asking. Suki had her moods and so did I. Each moment had to be met anew. My years with Suki were an ongoing lesson in how to get along on this earth. Now, when I'm not sure what's being asked of me and what to do next, I just lean in against the warm side of the living moment, reach underneath and feel my way along from there.

WITNESS:
AN EPILOGUE

I NO LONGER live on a farm, though I'm digging up a patch of backyard lawn to grow vegetables. And I don't now milk a cow in the morning; I walk in the park instead. At Cedar Grove, my route crosses a bridge spanning Chico Creek and turns downstream where I enter a grove of oaks in a field of grass. Passing under the oaks, I feel "witnessed" somehow, as if the oaks know I'm there. I say witnessed because "watched" is too specifically visual for the notice I feel I'm receiving. Oaks don't have eyes, and for that matter aren't considered sentient whatsoever. But I can't shake the feeling that they're conscious of my presence, though oaks aren't credited with consciousness either. And I don't credit them so; I don't believe in fairy tales or magic and am perfectly aware that imagination, while convincing within its own purlieu, is nonetheless only imagination with no necessary bearing on objective reality.

It's easily demonstrated that the gray squirrels, the woodpeckers, jays, robins, juncos, and titmice in the grove know I'm there. No one would doubt that; they're all sentient creatures after all. But is sentience really the limit of earth's witness to our human presence? Does nothing without sight, hearing, smell, or nerve endings to sense touch know that I'm here? Does the ground not register my footsteps, the air my breath, the grasses the shadow I cast upon them in the slant of morning light? I can remember the moment on that first morning when, contrary to all logical persuasion, I was convinced the oaks knew I was there, and that they knew so in the same direct way that cell knows cell within my earthly body.

Earth has been a long time coming to its present state. Has it never known itself to be orbiting the star that gave it birth and does that star not know its own circling child? And are we who are the offspring of molten rock not known by the parent soil that brought us forth? It's a long family story, and I'm not too sure that our siblings of plant, water, dirt, and air are so unconscious of our presence as we might think they are. Everywhere I go these days, I feel the reassuring witness of deep down things.

*related material
from other books
by Lin Jensen*

REAL ESTATE

Originally published in *Bad Dog! A Memoir of*
Love, Beauty, and Redemption in Hard Places

A MORNING in late May. Kneeling on the ground, I work a cultivator into the soil of the vegetable garden I tend here at our Sierra Valley home. The day warms, the shadows shorten toward noon. The soil turns up moist and dark beneath my hands.

All through the night while I slept, the planet revolved eastward, bearing this little western garden of mine back toward the sun, bearing the mountain night toward another day. The garden that comes to my hands today emerges out of a yesterday that traveled the distance of two vast oceans and three continents in its daily journey to the present.

The plot I cultivate is a raised bed four feet wide and twelve feet long. It is one of sixteen such beds in the garden. Like the others, it was dug and screened for rock. Its soil is rich with compost and earthworms. My digging here this morning releases the scent of warming soil.

The garden is fenced against the deer who come out of the

woods to feed in the open grassland where the garden is situated. Adjacent to the garden is a toolshed, a pump house, a well, and four compost bins. Down slope from the garden are a few apple trees and beyond these a house and garage finished in board and batten. The house opens onto a fenced yard landscaped with young trees and shrubs. A woodshed is joined to the garage. This household as I have described it sits on twenty acres of grassland sloping from a pine woods down to the county road below.

When Karen and I retired we bought this land. I know of course that it's perfectly ordinary to buy property. I can scoop up this garden earth and, though it is just a fistful of dirt like all the other dirt comprising these twenty acres of mine, even as I cup it in my hands, it is spinning in orbit round the sun. Nothing is holding still here. The whole place is in a state of rapid transit. This quickened soil that I hold in my hands owes its unlikely stability to sources as obscure as they are fantastic.

It is a dizzying proposition to think that I can own such a thing. Apparently I do, for such ownership is recognized in a joint tenancy grant deed issued by Cal-Sierra Title Company for Plumas County parcel number 025-420-10. But what can it really mean to "hold title" to so active a thing? What exactly is it that I own?

I ask these questions of myself because I know of no one else who will ask them of me. Yet they are questions that need to be asked. "Real estate" has become our most common designation for the earth upon which we live, and its fair market value has become the common measure of its worth. We think of land as property, a commodity for exchange. We ascribe to its ownership certain rights that we believe are due to us.

For four years now I have tended this garden. I broke the native sod and turned it under to rot. I screened the soil for rock and added manure hauled in from a neighbor's horse corral. I composted and watered and seeded and harvested and returned all waste to the ground. I have done these things, yet I have been helpless to effect any outcome except what the earth provides. And the earth provides not just a little, but all. The very body and mind with which I tend the earth are themselves of the earth. I am but earth tending earth. Were the earth not to roll this garden toward the sun today, were the clouds not to gather above the sea, the waters not to flow, the soil not to brim with its billions of microorganisms, were all or any part of this to fail, I would fail as well, my body numbed to a fixed stillness, my slightest thought cancelled.

This truth is so obvious that it is a wonder we can forget it so often and so easily. The fact of it defines who we are. To forget this is to forget who we are, a species suffering from amnesia that bewildered seeks its own name.

It is here in this garden that one can see how trivializing and irrelevant are the notions of property and property rights. This garden feeds me; it yields up life that I might have life. I am joined to this garden by an urgent interdependence. It is a salient, sacred, soul-sustaining fact that the best any of us can do is to harmonize our will to that of the earth. It is a teaching learned in humility and gratitude; it has no rights to press.

My body knows exactly how this stands; it taps not only into four years tending this garden but a lifetime bent to the task. Our bodies always know where we are even when we don't. Seasons rise and fall within us on blood tides of hunger. Daily need roots our mouths to the subsoil. When we lose sight of this, the fundamental wonder of it still lies fallow in our very tissues to be called forth again as joy.

This wonder, this springing joy, is our only health. Our sanity is measured by the presence in us of such wonder. Lose it, and we go mad. We deal in real estate. We become incoherent with talk of "property" and "title" and "rights pertaining to thereof."

I can survive the ownership of this mountain property with my mind intact if I never forget where I am and what I am doing. We humans have been entrusted to the earth, the earth entrusted to us. When we do not tune ourselves to this trust, the discord is fatal. Our only true song perishes on the instant, though we may seem to sing on endlessly.

DEFENDING EARTH

Orginially published in *Together Under One Roof: Making a Home of the Buddha's Household*

THERE ARISES from within the deeper meditations of Zen the realization that the surface of the skin is not a boundary between self and other. When that happens, the whole universe becomes an extension of self or, more accurately, the self becomes realized as an extension of the universe in an experience of integration so radical that Thich Nhat Hahn has coined the word *inter-being* to describe the condition. As a verb, it can be conjugated: I *inter-am*, she *inter-is*. We inter-are with all things—and this perception constitutes a radical environmentalism that argues a necessary defense of the earth. It is a defense that concurs with the Buddhist practice of nonharming. "All living things are one seamless body," an old scripture tells us. For the Zen Buddhist, this scripture is both a truth and an obligation. As a truth it's self-evident and can't easily be set aside. As an obligation, it guides our hand in all we do, for we realize that whatever we touch—sentient or non-sentient, scaled, feathered, furred, or fleshed—is one body, and that one body is our own.

Of course Buddhists have no monopoly on such feelings of connectedness. We humans are creatures of nature ourselves and have a deep and abiding affinity with the natural world. There must have been a time when we all recognized the earth and ourselves as extensions of one another, a time when our actions toward nature necessarily reflected the dependence and kinship we share with other creatures. Even now, this deeper realization must lie dormant somewhere beneath the tragic overlay of a century of human disregard of an abused, forgotten, and neglected earth. Buried beneath the successive and accumulating layers of sedimentary rock, it took ten hundred million years for the leaves that brushed the dinosaur's flanks to be pressed and heated into a lake of petroleum. Had we not chanced upon this vast reservoir of stored power things might have gone differently than they have. But with such unprecedented capabilities in hand, we unleashed the very force of nature *against* nature, measuring as gain an unspeakable and irreversible plundering of the land.

The proper defense of the earth is not found in protective custody but in relinquishment. What's needed most of all is the will to leave the earth alone and let it unfold in its own time and way. Ironically, wars—which are so often fought over who holds title to some disputed piece of land—are particularly destructive of land. In the aftermath of any modern war of sufficient scale, vast territories of countryside and city lie in ruins, poisoned by military ordinance of various sorts, and sometimes virtually uninhabitable for decades.

The actions of industry as well often comprise little less than a violent attack upon the earth. Factories belch poisonous carbon residues into the atmosphere until the surrounding skies darken and nearby mountains disappear. A yellowing sun glows dismally through the brown haze, and people cough and wheeze and look out through watering eyes. Frequent air pollution reports advise people, in regard for their health, to not go outdoors at all. The water of rivers that once ran clear and drinkable is rendered so poisonous by our human discharge that we would die of self-poisoning were we to drink it without first putting it through elaborate and costly water treatment procedures. The fish, with no such option, simply die off, leaving behind a river that is itself dead.

It's been our tragedy to forget where and by what means we live. Yet there are those among us who haven't forgotten; there are those who, because the earth can't speak for itself, have chosen to speak for it. And because the earth is ultimately vulnerable to the relentless pressures brought to bear upon it, there are those who will jeopardize the safety of their own lives in its protection.

In Thailand, Buddhist monks came to the defense of the nation's rainforests that had been brought to the edge of extinction by the logging interests of Western corporations. It so happened that the logging companies depended on village workers to cut down the trees. And while the villagers needed the work, they were also devotional Buddhists. So what the monks did was to enter the forests slated for logging where they performed ceremonies of ordination for several representative trees, chanting and draping the trees in ceremonial robes. The villagers, seeing the trees honored as Dharma brothers and sisters, refused to cut them down. To do so was seen as striking one's own flesh.

Those who have dedicated themselves to the defense of the earth have followed, with rare exception, a tradition of resistance that is nonviolent. In defense of the great whales, they have put themselves in the path of the whaler's harpoon; in defense of the rainforest, they have chained themselves to trees; in defense of the old-growth redwoods of the Pacific Northwest, they have climbed into the high branches and refused to return to ground for as long as two year's duration; in defense of wetlands and vernal pools, they have lain down in the path of the bulldozers. Their means of defense is to make themselves as vulnerable as the things they strive to protect, knowing that the body of earth is indivisible from their own.

Ultimately the defense of the earth is a defense of one's self.

Of all the municipal watersheds in this nation of ours, perhaps the most degraded of them is that of the Los Angeles Basin. The fifty-two mile length of the Los Angeles River that once meandered through a lush riparian corridor, spawning vast wetlands on its approach to the sea, has been reduced to a concrete drainage ditch stripped of all its vegetation, crisscrossed by a series of jammed freeways crawling with cars, lined by industrial plants, warehouses, and railroad yards. Backed up to the elevated cement levees and sandwiched between junkyards, gravel plants, and oil refineries are some of the poorest immigrant neighborhoods in the entire basin, remnants of what was once the original Pueblo de Los Angeles. Like the river, these inhabitants have been essentially discarded, put out of mind in favor of more profitable interests. But it is from these forgotten neighborhoods on the banks of this forgotten river that one of the most heartening defenses of the natural world has arisen.

They call themselves the River School, and they consist of middle school and high school students formed into teams to monitor what's left of the river in hopes of encouraging its unlikely restoration. Under the hum of high-voltage power lines and the sizzle of tires on an adjacent freeway, a group of teenagers with notebooks stand and look down the concrete inner slope of the levee to the floor of the river where the cement once laid down by the Army Corps of Engineers has cracked and split open to allow a trickle of stagnant water to ooze up out of the mud. A smear of green algae has gathered there and a few scrubby willows have taken root.

These children, deprived of contact with much of anything natural, find this small oasis in a degraded riverbed a thing of beauty. When they find a few crayfish clinging to the algae, they're thrilled with the discovery.

A thirteen-year-old named Brenda says, "My friends don't believe I went to the L.A. River! They're like, there's nothing there, that's a sewer! I used to think it was a sewer, too, but when I went there, it was beautiful." Another time she said, "The best bird I saw was the blue heron, a beautiful bird—I loved the blue." And the thing is, Brenda's right. The heron *is* beautiful. The slightest resurrection of nature under such unlikely circumstances is beautiful. And Brenda's delighted "I loved the blue" is as beautiful as it ever gets. Recalling a day when she and some others were tugging a heavy load of trash up out of the river channel, Brenda said, "I started to think, 'Oh my God, I could be cleaning up my own trash!' Gum or a piece of paper or something you threw out. It gave me a whole different look on the world." And Daniel, a classmate of Brenda's, said, "You can see plants coming through the cement—and that explains a lot. Nature is trying so very hard to be alive."

Nature *is* trying hard to be alive. And so are these offspring of the poverty-ridden, pavement-and-graffiti neighborhoods trying hard to be alive. They somehow know that their own survival is to be found in the resurrection and survival of the river.

The last frame of the Ten Ox-herding Pictures—a traditional series of teachings depicting the unfolding of the spiritual path— shows the newly enlightened bodhisattva re-entering the town of his birth with lifesaving hands, offering the joy and wisdom of his own awakening to any who choose to follow. Surely these enlightened youngsters descending into the scummy muck of what was once the Los Angeles River, clutching in their lifesaving hands an assortment of trash bags and notebooks, measuring sticks and sampling vials, are the bodhisattvas of our times. Their innocent delight in discovering there the least thing that still survives and grows is a measure of the heart's own native wisdom. Their seemingly hopeless undertaking to save the river measures the courage of the bodhisattva's vow to save all beings.

The River School volunteers beckon to us to follow. Their salvation, and ours, and that of the earth itself, depends on whether we will go with them or not.

INDEX

ABOUT THE AUTHOR

 LIN JENSEN is the author of *Together Under One Roof*; *Pavement*, which chronicled his experiences as a protester for peace; and *Bad Dog!*—all of which were *Shambhala Sun* "Best Buddhist Writing" selections. He is Senior Buddhist Chaplain at High Desert State Prison in Susanville, California, and the founder and teacher of the Chico Zen Sangha, in Chico, California, where he lives with his wife, Karen.

ABOUT WISDOM PUBLICATIONS

To LEARN MORE ABOUT WISDOM PUBLICATIONS, a nonprofit publisher, and to browse our other books dedicated to skillful living, visit our website at www.wisdompubs.org. You may request a copy of our catalog online or by writing to this address:

Wisdom Publications
199 Elm Street
Somerville, Massachusetts 02144 USA
Telephone: 617-776-7416
Fax: 617-776-7841
Email: info@wisdompubs.org
www.wisdompubs.org

Wisdom is a nonprofit, charitable 501(c)(3) organization affiliated with the Foundation for the Preservation of the Mahayana Tradition (FPMT).